Special Snowflake Syndrome:

The Unrecognized Personality Disorder

Destroying the World

Heather Silvio, PsyD

Panther Books

Published in the United States by Panther Books, Las Vegas.

Contact the publisher at:
information@pantherbooks.us

Correspondence to the author may be sent to:
hlsilvio@yahoo.com

Cover design by Lori Malkin Ehrlich
Headshot by Sidney Oster Photography

This is a work of nonfiction. Information contained is based on the author's experiences as a human and clinical psychologist. Sources are provided for non-public domain information. Quotes are from public sources/people not personally known to the author; the use of the quotes/sources does not imply endorsement by those individuals of this book. Individuals specifically mentioned in the book as behaving consistent with a special snowflake have not been evaluated by me and have not been diagnosed in any way by me.

ISBN (Print) 978-0-9908005-6-9 / 0-9908005-6-3
ISBN (E-book) 978-0-9908005-7-6 / 0-9908005-7-1

ALSO BY HEATHER SILVIO

Paranormal Talent Agency (Books 1-6)

Happiness by the Numbers:
9 Steps to Authentic Happiness

Not Quite Famous:
A Romantic Comedy of an Actress on the Edge

Beyond the Abyss:
Tales of the Supernatural

Stress Disorders:
A Healing Path for PTSD

Courting Death

CONTENTS

ACKNOWLEDGMENTS

To all the special snowflakes.

INTRODUCTION

Or WARNING: THIS BOOK MAY OFFEND!

What is Special Snowflake Syndrome and why is it dooming the human race?

You may or may not have heard the terms special snowflake, Generation Snowflake, or Special Snowflake Syndrome. If you have heard of them, you may or may not know exactly what they mean. When I had the idea for this book, I did a ton of research and discovered that, despite its prevalence, people were writing about special snowflakes in a very narrow way. Other than occasional articles, the best book I found was Claire Fox's *I Find that Offensive* (2016), written about Generation Snowflake, a good, but limited look at what I will be detailing as a broader societal problem.

Until now, nobody has written a book defining Special Snowflake Syndrome, including detailing its origins, psychological features, dangers, and cure. That's where this book plans to fill the gap.

Special Snowflake Syndrome: The Unrecognized Personality Disorder Destroying the World is presented in two parts:

Part I: What is Special Snowflake Syndrome?
Part II: Curing Special Snowflake Syndrome

In the first part, I provide the origins of the term Special Snowflake Syndrome. Then, based on my experience as a clinical psychologist, I detail my psychological definition and criteria for the unofficial personality disorder of Special Snowflake Syndrome. Unofficial because Special Snowflake Syndrome is *not* a diagnosable disorder at this time. Given its prevalence across all segments of society and its dangers to the whole of society, I consider it worth presenting as a diagnosable condition from a psychological perspective, but also as a form of social commentary. The remainder of Part I will be on the dangers of Special Snowflake Syndrome to the individual and society.

So as not to unhelpfully explain why the world is going to hell in a hand basket (as I keep hearing) and leave everybody depressed, Part II focuses on ways to cure ourselves of Special Snowflake Syndrome and, thus, save the world.

I divide Part II into three sections: assuming benevolence, taking others' perspectives, and recognizing it's okay to fail (despite what people in the age of the participation trophy have learned). The techniques in Part II can be used by any individuals with the insight to recognize they have Special Snowflake Syndrome, and can also be modeled by those in the lives of these individuals. Both can help reduce the distress and negative impact of Special Snowflake Syndrome.

Each chapter in both parts concludes with a brief summary of the major points of the chapter, including space for you to make notes on what you've read. In Part II, the chapter conclusions also include a brief reminder of how to implement the recommended strategies for curing Special Snowflake Syndrome.

The book finishes with my Final Thoughts on where we've been and where we're going. My goal by the end of *Special Snowflake Syndrome: The Unrecognized Personality Disorder Destroying the World* is to demonstrate the role we each play in making the world a place where we all want to live, where we can be happy, and where we can support each other.

We can do it!

Oh, and remember my warning that this book may offend…

It is likely that everybody will be offended by something I've written because I don't present an ideological "side" and I ask everyone to challenge themselves. My examples are largely ripped from the headlines and cross all political and ideological lines.

You have been warned!

A quick note – although I use real-world examples, I specifically avoid the use of names for two reasons. One, the examples are about the behavior not the person. And two, since I have not met or evaluated anybody whose behavior I call out in this book, I therefore have not diagnosed them with anything.

PART I

WHAT IS SPECIAL SNOWFLAKE SYNDROME?

DR HEATHER SILVIO

1 ORIGINS OF THE TERM

In order to cure the world of Special Snowflake Syndrome, first must come an understanding of what is meant by the term and the dangers it poses. This first chapter presents the background on the origins of the expression Special Snowflake Syndrome, as well as related terms that preceded or developed alongside it.

Special Snowflake Syndrome followed from the phrase, special snowflake, and is a broader version of the term, Generation Snowflake. Let's look at these first.

Special Snowflake

1) According to the website knowyourmeme.com (2015, para 1), "**Special Snowflake** is a derogatory term widely used on Tumblr to describe someone who often whines about deserving special treatment or sees oneself

as exceptionally unique for no apparent reason, similar to the use of the expression **check your privilege** in the social justice blogosphere." [emphasis included from the original source].

2) According to urbandictionary.com (2015, para 1), "The Special Snowflake (Also referred to as one with the 'Special Snowflake Syndrome' or 'SSS') is a person who believes they are different and unique from everyone else because of something there [sic] are or do."

Generation Snowflake

According to urbandictionary.com (2016, para 1), Generation Snowflake can be defined as, "The group of young people today that have the INSANE belief they have the right to NOT be offended by any of the beliefs/viewpoints of the other 7.1 billion people of this planet. When these fragile/infantile people are offended, most likely they will react in someway [sic] like a toddler (cry, scream, act hysterical, etc)."

Special Snowflake Syndrome

Of the four submitted definitions of Special Snowflake Syndrome on urbandictionary.com (2011, para 1-4), the first one is the most thorough and helpful:

"A malady affecting a significant portion of the world's population wherein the afflicted will demand special treatment, conduct themselves with a ludicrous, unfounded sense of **entitlement**, and generally make the lives of everyone around them that much more miserable. The danger of this disease is that the sufferers rarely, if ever, know that they have contracted it, and continue about their merry way under the assumption that EVERYONE ELSE is the problem. This condition, if left untreated, can radically alter the carrier's demeanor, to include any of the following: a complete devolution to child-like behavior, temper tantrums, and/or fits of **narcissistic** rage. When confronted with an individual suspected of harboring Special Snowflake Syndrome, one's best course of action is to run away. Further attempts at educating the carrier on the reality of their condition (e.g., quoting **Tyler Durden**: 'You are not special. You are not a beautiful or unique snowflake. You're the same decaying organic matter as everything else.') will likely prove futile, and potentially hazardous to the informer." [emphasis included from the original source].

What I would add is that while all people are self-interested to a given extent (and this is likely hardwired for survival), there is a definite line between self-interest and development of Special Snowflake Syndrome.

Where does the term Special Snowflake Syndrome come from? This is actually not so easily answered. Going back to the beginning, as noted in the definition above, the first sort-of reference was widely heard in the 1999 movie "Fight Club" (screenplay by Jim Uhls, based on the 1996 novel by Chuck Palahniuk) where the character of Tyler Durden utters the following: "Listen up, maggots. You are not special. You are not a beautiful or unique snowflake. You're the same decaying organic matter as everything else."

Somebody took that quote and it became "special snowflake", "snowflake syndrome", and "special snowflake syndrome". According to knowyourmeme.com (2015), the terms began to spread online through sites like LiveJournal and Tumblr, before going fully mainstream on sites like Yahoo Answers and urbandictionary.com. The two examples listed below typify the sporadic mentions:

In 2008, aloha.girl59 asks the question in Yahoo Answers, "What is 'Special Snowflake Syndrome'?" The top answer directs her to urbandictionary.com.

One mention of 'Snowflake Syndrome' appears in a 2009 online blog at NYC Educator. In it, the author Miss Eyre writes about her experiences with special snowflake middle school students.

So what is Special Snowflake Syndrome? A special snowflake is someone who believes they are unique in the world and deserving of special treatment. It becomes the full-blown Special Snowflake Syndrome when it is consistently reflected in the person's thoughts, words, and actions. In other words, a person can be said to have Special Snowflake Syndrome when they consistently believe they are unique, entitled, and unable to see another person's perspective, and thus elevate their own needs above everyone else's.

Personality Disorder

While I largely agree with what has come before this book, there are two key beliefs I have that differentiate my clinical opinion (and therefore, this book) from what has come before.

1) Special Snowflake Syndrome is not **solely** generational. Many of the references to special snowflakes, Generation Snowflake, and Special Snowflake Syndrome declare that this is an issue of the Millennial – typically defined as an individual born from the late-70s/early 80s to the 1990s (Noren, 2011). Yes, Special Snowflake Syndrome is heavily represented in the Millennial generation at present. But, I believe the issue is more complex, and believe this is due to three things

11

(addressed more fully later in the book). One, a slight misperception based on the fact that the young are often louder than older generations (regardless of the opinions they hold) and the omnipresence of social media results in **everyone** hearing about all the opinions and antics of the Millennials. Two, while I do agree full blown Special Snowflake Syndrome developed with the Millennials, the parents of the Millennials likely had traits of special snowflakes first. And, three, I don't believe that when the Millenials "grow up" they will suddenly mature and the attitudes/behaviors will dissipate; I think we're seeing the tip of the iceberg, as they say. I believe that there will be individuals across all generations afflicted with Special Snowflake Syndrome.

2) Special Snowflake Syndrome has grown beyond an amusing and disparaging moniker to a full-fledged personality disorder for some. According to the most recent edition of the Diagnostic and Statistical Manual of Mental Disorders (DSM-5, 2013, pg. 645), "a personality disorder is an enduring pattern of inner experience and behavior that deviates markedly from the expectations of the individual's culture, is pervasive and inflexible, has an onset in adolescence or early adulthood, is stable over time, and leads to distress or impairment". I will make the case that Special Snowflake Syndrome meets this standard for a certain (as yet unknown) percentage of the population.

Note that a worry expressed by some (e.g., Fox, 2013) is that by pathologizing the ups and downs of everyday life as mental illness, we risk increasing the over-reactivity that is of concern. However, almost by definition, as I will show in the next chapter, when ways of thinking, feeling, and behaving become the all-encompassing approach one uses across all aspects of life, and develops into an enduring/inflexible unhelpful pattern, then this typically meets criteria for a mental health disorder diagnosis! And, in that case, it **is** quite appropriate to reference this in that manner. I definitely agree that the use of the word "trauma" has been quite overblown – and I even discuss this in my own book on posttraumatic stress disorder (Silvio, 2013). BUT, this is about the overall picture. And for a segment of society, it's a scary one.

The next chapter in Part I will lay out the **Psychological Features** of Special Snowflake Syndrome as a personality disorder as I am defining it.

Chapter One Summary

Special Snowflake Syndrome developed from the terms special snowflake and Generation Snowflake.

Special Snowflake Syndrome afflicts primarily Millennials, but that is just the tip of the iceberg.

Special Snowflake Syndrome has become a full fledged (albeit as yet unofficial) personality disorder for some.

Notes

2 PSYCHOLOGICAL FEATURES

Based on the formatting of diagnoses in the DSM-5 (2013), my unofficial diagnosis, Special Snowflake Syndrome, will adhere to the same format. I've already explained why I believe it to be a personality disorder. I further believe Special Snowflake Syndrome would specifically fall under the Cluster B personality disorders, "individuals with these disorders often appear dramatic, emotional, or erratic" (DSM-5, pg. 646).

My Proposed Diagnostic Criteria

A pervasive pattern of disregard for others, lack of empathy, grandiosity, and hypersensitivity, beginning by early adulthood and present in a variety of contexts, as indicated by 5 (or more) of the following:

1. Frequent demanding of special treatment regardless of circumstances.

2. Sense of entitlement or unrealistic expectation of favorable treatment from others regardless of deservedness.

3. Elevation of their needs above others, regardless of the objective importance of those needs, or the impact on others.

4. Inability to recognize the perspectives of others, or to consider that the opinions of others may have validity.

5. Easily offended by others' words and behaviors, especially if triggered by perceived injustice.

6. Displaying developmentally inappropriate behavior in response to perceived disagreeable actions of others.

7. Inappropriate and/or intense displays of anger, often in the form of a narcissistic rage.

8. Believes others are the sole source of any problem, negative emotion, or poor outcome.

Diagnostic Features

The essential feature of Special Snowflake Syndrome is a pervasive pattern of disregard for others, lack of empathy, grandiosity, and hypersensitivity that begins by early adulthood and is present in a variety of contexts.

Individuals with Special Snowflake Syndrome frequently demand special treatment regardless of circumstances (Criterion 1). They demand others provide what they believe they deserve and thus, this is usually tied to their sense of entitlement (Criterion 2). However, this moves beyond simply asking for additional unwarranted consideration, and includes actively unrealistic expectations of favorable treatment from others regardless of deservedness.

Because these individuals believe they are special and unique, this often results in an elevation of their needs above others, regardless of the objective importance of those needs, or the impact on others (Criterion 3). They routinely believe they are more important than others, whether friends, family, or strangers.

Individuals with this disorder demonstrate an inability to recognize the perspectives of others, or to consider that the opinions of others may have validity (Criterion 4). They are horribly shocked by any disagreement with others, often also resulting in being easily offended by others' words and behaviors, especially if triggered by perceived injustice (Criterion 5). If an individual with Special Snowflake Syndrome believes they are righting a wrong, they will likely appear inflexible with those beliefs.

Given their belief in their moral superiority, individuals with this disorder will display developmentally inappropriate behavior in response to perceived disagreeable actions of others (Criterion 6). If someone disagrees with them, they may break down in tears or yell, out of proportion to the inciting event. This often appears as inappropriate and/or intense displays of anger, often in the form of a narcissistic rage (Criterion 7).

Finally, individuals with Special Snowflake Syndrome, directly related to the above criteria, believe others are the sole source of any problem, negative emotion, or poor outcome (Criterion 8). Because of this intensely held belief, these individuals can be difficult to reason with, may be unable to compromise, and may be completely unable to see the role their own beliefs and/or behavior may have played in a given situation. This makes it quite difficult for the individual to change their thoughts, emotions, or behaviors.

Associated Features Supporting Diagnosis

Individuals with Special Snowflake Syndrome display a seemingly contradictory presentation of fragility of self with a brazen sense of self-importance. They believe strongly in their convictions, which usually place themselves center-stage, and are hypersensitive to disagreement. This need to have total agreement combined with over-the-top reactions to disagreement often results in attempts to control others' expression of opinions. On college campuses, for example, this can be seen in the creation of "safe spaces" [discussed later] where people are expected to speak only approved opinions; on social media, this can be seen by people "unfriending" or shaming anyone who disagrees with them; and in day-to-day life, this can be seen when someone says, "I find that offensive!" to stop the other person from speaking.

Prevalence

Since Special Snowflake Syndrome is not yet officially a diagnosis, there have been no studies evaluating prevalence in the population. According to the DSM-5 (2013), the prevalence estimates are "1.5% for disorders in Cluster B [...] and 9.1% for any personality disorder" (pg. 646). Special Snowflake Syndrome likely has similar percentages. It may seem higher due to the media coverage of certain outbursts and overreactions of those with the Syndrome.

Development and Course

I use a three-strikes-and-you're-out metaphor to describe the development of Special Snowflake Syndrome within the population as a whole, as well as within specific individuals.

Our first strike against us is from an evolutionary perspective. Without getting too technical, human beings are hard-wired for a certain level of self-interest as a survival mechanism. And this is generally a good thing, because it allows us to look out for ourselves to ensure our continued existence. Now, typically, it also extends beyond our own person to others in our community, part of what later we called a social contract. True survival depended on moving beyond simple self-interest to community interest. So this genetic degree of self-interest has been and is largely a positive attribute – it wasn't until we moved into the second strike that we began to see problems.

Unfortunately, the second strike against us began to reduce that genuine community interest. Sorry, parents. This strike is on you to a large extent:

- Trying to **just** be your child's friend.
- Telling them repeatedly that they're special, unique, and perfect.
- Placing their self-esteem (which **is** important, but not **all**-important) above everything else.
- And, most damaging of all, acting as a helicopter parent, not allowing them to fail by (inaccurately) teaching them that the world will universally respond to their amazing uniqueness.

As I'll expand upon in a later section, it's likely that some parents already developed traits of Special Snowflake Syndrome; their parenting style then exaggerated this for their children.

The third strike against us that can lead to full-blown Special Snowflake Syndrome for a subset of the population is the incredible proliferation of social media that:

- Encourages the vocalization of the special interest group to the exclusion of other groups and, frankly, common sense.
- Confirms (or at least gives the illusion) that the "public" waits with bated breath for their every comment, question, and (especially) complaint about the world.
- Again tells them that they're unique, special, and should not fail.
- If they do fail, it is someone else's "fault".

By the third strike, an individual is more likely to develop Special Snowflake Syndrome and become a problem, not just to themselves, but to the people around them.

What we are seeing with Special Snowflake Syndrome is that for a subset of the population: genetics predispose them to self-interest; their parents shaped that self-interest to be exaggerated and unrealistic; and, finally, social media seemingly confirmed their specialness and encouraged externalizing blame for all problems onto others. Society created Special Snowflake Syndrome.

Regarding the course of Special Snowflake Syndrome, this is further hypothesizing, due to the newness of the Syndrome and the lack of longitudinal studies. There are likely two courses the Syndrome can take.

If the individual succeeds in closing off all dissenting opinions, they likely will remain quite sheltered with symptoms unabated. Outside of this bubble of belief, they will increasingly display an impaired ability to participate in an appropriate social manner with those of differing opinions and views on the world.

The second course the Syndrome can take results if the individual is unable to maintain their "safe space" bubble in all facets of their lives (school/work, home, and relationships) and continues to be confronted by individuals who do not agree with them. In this instance, the individual will likely experience significant distress, possibly daily distress. They then most likely may either stay miserable or try to create the artificial safe space bubble described in the first possible course. With proper treatment, they could begin to confront and challenge their problematic thoughts, emotional reactions, and interpersonal functioning.

Risk and Prognostic Factors

Genetic and Physiological. Pure conjecture again, since this is not an established diagnosis. Given that the presence of diagnosed mental health disorders in the family typically increases the likelihood of an individual's development of that or a similar disorder, this likely would also be the case for Special Snowflake Syndrome.

Temperamental. Factors predicting risk and/or prognosis of Special Snowflake Syndrome have not been definitively characterized. Certainly, youthful age and studying at university have been labeled as factors. This may reflect reporting style, resulting in social commentators missing examples of Special Snowflake Syndrome in other-than-Millennial generations. Because many have decided this is solely a generational issue, when older adults engage in behavior suggestive of Special Snowflake Syndrome, it is misattributed to some other unrelated factor. For example, an elderly white male shooting another man in a movie theater over texting would not be attributed to Special Snowflake Syndrome, but if other criteria are met, it certainly could be an example of the personality disorder, though the media would be unlikely to attribute the actions to the disorder – and in fact did not (Almasy, 2014). Of course, this behavior may simply be an overreaction to the individuals with Special Snowflake Syndrome themselves; non-Millennials choosing not to filter their responses anymore because they're tired of what they see around them. Future research could better clarify.

Culture-Related Diagnostic Issues

The pattern of thoughts, emotions, and behaviors characteristic of Special Snowflake Syndrome, thus far, seems concentrated in America, the United Kingdom, and other developed countries. This again may reflect merely a reporting issue, or more likely because in other parts of the world, there are genuine issues on which to focus (such as genital mutilation or even just having access to clean water).

Gender-Related Diagnostic Issues

There is no consensus regarding gender of individuals with symptoms of Special Snowflake Syndrome (including special snowflakes and members of Generation Snowflake). Some express the belief that females are more likely to exhibit the symptoms (e.g., urbandictionary.com, #3, 2014), while others (like myself) believe it exists across genders. For example, in some of the videos and stories I'll discuss later in the book, males are certainly involved in the situations and behave consistent with Special Snowflake Syndrome.

Differential Diagnosis

Other personality disorders and personality traits. Special Snowflake Syndrome has varying degrees of overlap with the diagnoses of Borderline (e.g., inappropriate intense anger) and, especially, Narcissistic (e.g., belief that one is special or unique) personality disorders. As the DSM-5 (2013) states, however, "it is therefore important to distinguish among these disorders based on differences in their characteristic features" remembering of course, that "all can be diagnosed" if the individual meets criteria for more than one (pg 662). The key then will be looking at the individual's presentation in total to determine if the proposed criteria for Special Snowflake Syndrome have been met.

Immaturity. Beyond considering other diagnoses, it will also be important to simply consider developmental immaturity. Many people exhibit some of the Special Snowflake Syndrome traits at varying times of life, and certainly the immaturity of adolescents and young adults marks them as likely to display a number of the criteria listed above. Therefore, it is important to wait until able to determine that the traits have become a pattern and "the enduring pattern is inflexible and pervasive across a broad range of personal and social situations [...that ...] leads to clinically significant distress or impairment in social, occupational, or other important areas of functioning" (DSM-5, 2013, pg 646).

Do I have Special Snowflake Syndrome?

Reading that last section may have felt quite technical, so let's break it down into everyday language with specific examples. Who might have Special Snowflake Syndrome? If you have concerns that you or someone around you has Special Snowflake Syndrome, ask yourself a few questions first:

- Does the person become angry or upset when others don't agree with them?
- Does the person always have to be right?
- Are they easily offended?
- Does the person believe that people do not recognize their greatness?
- Do they break down over the smallest disappointment or criticism?

Two additional questions:

- If the answers to the above questions are "no", would the other people in their lives agree?
- Can you imagine them already arguing with me and becoming defensive?

Let's look at this a third way. How often do you or the other person utter the following phrases?

"But, I'm right!"
"I'm entitled to my opinion."

A quick note: If you're beginning to wonder about yourself, before you start to argue with me (or worse, stop reading the book!), let me clarify. Like I wrote above, we are looking for **patterns** in thoughts and behaviors. Everyone is absolutely entitled to their opinion; we all get angry sometimes; and we don't have to enjoy receiving criticism. However, if you find yourself demonstrating the above repeatedly, it may go beyond the occasional flights of self-interest, and you may suffer from Special Snowflake Syndrome.

How is this different than just being a jerk?

Although I ask the above question somewhat facetiously, this could be a legitimate question if you're considering a single example of one specific behavior. That's part of why I've mentioned before and will mention again that we're looking for patterns. Sometimes people have an off day. Sometimes we may hit on their hot button issue and they're inflexible. Sometimes people are miserable in their own lives and take that out on other people. That doesn't mean they would meet criteria for Special Snowflake Syndrome.

And that's the answer to the question. Consider what you've read above. In order to be "diagnosed" with Special Snowflake Syndrome, the following would have to be true:

- Meet five out of the eight specific criteria
- Experience significant negative impact across the major life areas

In addition, I think one component that may turn out to be fairly important is how the individual with Special Snowflake Syndrome reacts when they're activated. Someone who's **just** self-centered, or **just** over-reactive, or **just** hypersensitive likely will be miserable but stay relatively self-contained. The **Associated Feature** of the individual with Special Snowflake Syndrome taking it to the next level by trying to exert power to force change and actually impact society in a significant negative way (e.g., shutting down free speech) may turn out to be a critical component.

If you're unsure whether or not you or the people around you have Special Snowflake Syndrome, let's look at some real-world cases exemplifying the specific signs detailed in the proposed criteria spelled out above. Remember, we're looking for examples in our thoughts, words, and actions of the signs of Special Snowflake Syndrome. Note that for many of the examples, they demonstrate more than just the one criterion for which I'm using them as the example:

1. Frequent demanding of special treatment regardless of circumstances.

You enroll in a program of study at a university. As you look over the courses you're required to take, you see a few that you'd rather not, whether because of lack of interest, lack of perceived ability, or some other reason. What do you do?

If you're like most students, if the courses are required for your program of study, you suck it up and take the classes. For a group of students at Yale University, however, because they found certain courses offensive, they demanded the special treatment of being excused from taking them (Campbell, 2016). What makes this an example of demanding special treatment? These are students enrolled in a program of study ostensibly to earn a degree in English and they are objecting to two classes studying "Major English Poets" due to the lack of representation by women, people of color, and gays. As the author of the article points out: in England, historically, the majority of the poets were white men.

As a female writer, I certainly understand the desire to see people fully represented. But, demanding to be released from classes that are part of the course of study the students signed up for because they are offended by the inclusion of white male poets (and who are in fact some of the literary giants of the past)...those students might be special snowflakes.

2. Sense of entitlement or unrealistic expectation of favorable treatment from others regardless of deservedness.

Consider campus or work life. You go to the cafeteria and try a couple of different meals. Some you like and some you don't. Maybe you'd like it if they had something healthier, presented more vegetarian options, or offered more variety overall. What would you expect the school or company to do about it?

In a story out of Oberlin College, the students there not only objected to the cafeteria workers' attempts to make a greater variety of food, but charged that the inauthentic versions of various ethnic foods were actually offensive (Soave, 2015; Licea & Italiano, 2015). Various students protested verbally and/or physically about the General Tso's chicken, banh mi sandwiches, fried chicken, etc not being cooked correctly; they actually described it as "insensitive", "culturally inappropriate", "ridiculous", and "disrespectful" (Licea & Italiano, 2015, para 1, 5, and 6). This is a textbook example of a sense of entitlement and unrealistic expectations. How could the students expect that the cafeteria workers would know how to make every dish exactly the way it would have been made in the students' interpretations of their various cultures? And why do the students believe they are entitled to it to begin with?

This sign of Special Snowflake Syndrome often reflects many aspects of the other criteria for the proposed diagnosis. If an individual frequently becomes frustrated by others not agreeing with them, not giving them what they want when they want it, and feeling like a victim for not receiving what they believe they are entitled to – and they respond by complaining and protesting over the unrealistic expectations not being met – then they may be a special snowflake.

3. Elevation of their needs above others, regardless of the objective importance of those needs, or the impact on others.

You're sitting in a theater watching the latest comic book movie and your phone vibrates, informing you that someone is calling or texting. What do you do?

Most people would give the "correct" answer of, you ignore it. Except that social media and our personal experience abound with examples of people answering the call or text. This is a basic example of the Special Snowflake Syndrome sign of elevating your needs above others. There have been several high profile examples in recent years of individuals with Special Snowflake Syndrome answering these calls and/or texts and proceeding to have full verbal or texting conversations. Lin-Manuel Miranda, writer and star of the Broadway show *Hamilton*, indirectly called out a famous celebrity for frequent texting during his show (Fox News Latino, 2015), and Patti LuPone actually confiscated a texting audience member's phone (Leopold, 2015).

In the theater, whether live theater or a movie, being on your phone, whether taking a call, texting, or illegally recording the performance, are all examples of Special Snowflake Syndrome behavior. Someone engaging in any of those behaviors, and needing to justify their actions…they may be a special snowflake.

4. Inability to recognize the perspectives of others, or to consider that the opinions of others may have validity.

You are a teacher of a particular topic. For one of your classes, you have typically presented both sides of the issues. This political season, though, you find the differences between Hillary Clinton and Donald Trump are too egregious. Do you change your presentation?

This is the flip side of elevating your needs above others; failing to consider another person's perspective. If you're an associate professor of political science at one college, you write in an opinion piece stating, "it is a disservice to students to attempt to provide balance when I know that balance is an offense to the truth" (Ianello, 2016, para 13). Her role as an educator is to provide information and guide students to exploring, including to ideas different than hers, and yet, in her own words, she states doing so is offensive, clearly demonstrating the Special Snowflake Syndrome sign of inability to consider that the opinions of others may have validity.

What about students in her classes who support the other candidate? In an interview, she insisted, "I can assure you that all students will have a voice in my classes" (Lopez, 2016, para 6). However, in that same article, the professor is described by a student as "not open to new ideas and is very close minded on her beliefs" (Lopez, 2016, para 9). When you demonstrate the inability to recognize the perspectives of others, you may be a special snowflake. Just about any time a person feels the need to justify their behavior, they probably ought not to engage in the behavior.

5. Easily offended by others' words and behaviors, especially if triggered by perceived injustice.

You're driving to work and you see a billboard with a fit woman in a bikini staring back at you. The words, "Are you beach-body ready?" jump out at you. What do you think and how do you feel? What do you do about it?

This is a perfect example of the hypersensitivity of people. The politically correct response is to cry, "fat shaming", and demand the billboard be removed (which is exactly what happened in one example in Britain; Crocker, 2015). However, the mature response to this is to not care because it doesn't actually matter in your life. If a billboard upsets you enough to start a petition to remove it, or you are someone who would sign that petition, and you believe that you are standing up for others in the fat shaming "war", I'm sorry to say that you may be a special snowflake.

Please don't send me any hate mail, but this is a great example of people becoming easily offended by something that does not genuinely impact them in any meaningful form. It's a fitness model. In a bikini. So what?

The fact is that we will always encounter people and opinions that we do not share – and some words and behaviors certainly may be genuinely offensive. But many are not. The expectation that because you have cried, "this is offensive", that it'll instantly be changed, points toward being a special snowflake. If you are unable to simply ignore something you don't like, you create your own distress.

6. Displaying developmentally inappropriate behavior in response to perceived disagreeable actions of others.

You're following all the political posts on social media, watching countless news stories about dire predictions if a particular presidential candidate wins. If your preferred candidate doesn't win, are you moving to Canada?

If you laughed at my question, you're probably not a special snowflake. If you didn't, pay close attention. Seriously declaring you're moving to Canada (or any other location outside the United States) if your preferred presidential candidate does not win, is a developmentally inappropriate response to the perceived disagreeable actions of others. It's the political equivalent of, "I don't like what you did, so I'm not playing with you anymore. I'm taking my ball and going home". In case you made assumptions about which candidates and which presidential race I'm referring to, check this out. In 2012, some conservatives threatened to move to Canada if Barack Obama won reelection (McLaughlin, 2012) and some liberals threatened to move if he didn't (Bowman, 2012). This political season, you have both sides again claiming they will move, anywhere from Canada or Costa Rica to Ireland or Mexico based on the outcome of the election (Carroll, 2016).

Obviously, we don't have to all agree on everything. Frankly, life would be pretty boring if that was the case. On the other hand, if someone responds in childish ways to behaviors of others and outcomes they don't like, they may be a special snowflake.

7. Inappropriate and/or intense displays of anger, often in the form of a narcissistic rage.

You attend a presentation by someone with whom you do not particularly agree. You raise your hand to comment, make one or two statements, and the presenter moves on to the next question or portion of his/her talk. What do you do?

Most people, again, will give the "correct" answer of either continuing to listen respectfully, or leave the room, having said what they came to say. In real life, what instead we sometimes see is a full-blown childish temper tantrum. Perhaps you remember the story (and video) of one university student literally having a complete melt down during, of all things, a free speech event. She is the poster child of the Special Snowflake Syndrome sign of displaying temper tantrums, yelling and flailing her arms exactly like a child throwing a tantrum in a store because mommy won't buy her a candy bar (Campus Reform, 2016).

In an extreme case of Criterion 6, we get Criterion 7, the temper tantrum. If someone finds themselves actually screaming and crying because somebody else is disagreeing with them or because they believe they have not been heard to their satisfaction...they may be a special snowflake.

8. Believes others are the sole source of any problem, negative emotion, or poor outcome.

I saved this final sign for last because it is the most insidious and makes resolving all of the others that much more difficult. Why might this be? Because if everyone else is the problem, then I will expect everyone else to change before I ever look inward to see my responsibility.

There are many, many examples of this denial of responsibility. We see it everywhere from our language ("I have to do ____" rather than "I choose to do ____") to our actions ("I want a safe space, therefore you are not allowed to express any views contrary to my own").

I see it expressed personally, when people play the victim, blaming others for their undesirable outcomes and lack of success. I see it expressed professionally, when people blame other departments or coworkers for not performing to standards. I see it expressed emotionally, when people blame others for their own unhappiness.

Failing to take responsibility and expecting everyone around you to change in order for you to be happy and fulfilled is the greatest challenge of Special Snowflake Syndrome because you have instantly become the victim, unable or unwilling to help yourself. And if we all approach life this way…if everyone else is always the problem…what are we left with?

A bunch of whiny, fragile, self-absorbed adult-sized children incapable of working together to help each other and build a sense of community. And that leads me into the chapter on the **Dangers** of Special Snowflake Syndrome.

Chapter Two Summary

Psychological features of the proposed personality disorder Special Snowflake Syndrome, including:

My Proposed Diagnostic Criteria

Diagnostic Features

Associated Features

Prevalence

Development and Course

Risk and Prognostic Factors

Culture- and Gender-Related Diagnostic Issues

Differential Diagnosis

Questions to ask if you suspect either you (or someone around you) may have Special Snowflake Syndrome.

Examples of each of the Proposed Criteria of Special Snowflake Syndrome, including why they represent that particular criterion of the disorder.

Notes

3 DANGERS

Why care about Special Snowflake Syndrome? Unfortunately, the impact of Special Snowflake Syndrome is real and far-reaching. We hopefully all care because there are dangerous negative consequences to the spread of Special Snowflake Syndrome. This next part will largely focus on the United States, since that is where I live, but understand that Special Snowflake Syndrome is, sadly, not a uniquely American problem. It seems to exist certainly in similar Western cultures, such as Australia and the United Kingdom (e.g., Fox, 2013).

In addition, although Millennials seem to be the first to disproportionately demonstrate the Syndrome, it's not due to simple immaturity and youthful narcissism. They likely won't just grow out of it, or be the last, unless something is done to stop the continuation of their destructiveness, stop the creation of additional generations, and stop the formation of a tyrannical state that such individuals seem hell-bent on creating (for the greater good, of course!)

The dangers of Special Snowflake Syndrome thus begin first with dangerous psychological consequences for the individual. This then creates a bigger impact sociologically with dangerous negative consequences for society. Finally, all this pandering to the special snowflakes results in extreme political consequences, including the dangers of creating thought police or even a police state. What exactly does all this look like? I'm sure you'll recognize much of what I write next.

Dangerous Individual Consequences

Special Snowflake Syndrome is creating a nation of self-perceived victims. The negative psychological impact of this on individuals cannot be overstated. College students afraid to leave their homes for fear someone will say something mean to them; protesters shutting down free speech they disagree with; and an inability to deal with any criticism or listen to any opinions/viewpoints that differ from their own. Psychologically, by taking into account everybody's feelings, we're actually becoming much less tolerant. **Agree with me or be vilified!**

Four areas I want to address under the individual consequences include the rise of mental health issues, tragedy of microaggressions, tyranny of safe spaces, and "why shouldn't I have it my way?". You will see how these can result from and reinforce the hypersensitivity, over-reactivity, and narcissism of an individual with Special Snowflake Syndrome.

Poor Mental Health and Suicide

One of the required characteristics of a personality disorder is that it results in significant distress across multiple life spheres, as I noted in the last chapter. There are concerns being expressed regarding the possible increase in mental health issues in youth (Marshall, 2016; Buckland, 2016), and I suspect at least some of that is related to special snowflake traits and full-blown Special Snowflake Syndrome.

Last chapter, I indicted social media for the negative impact it has directly had on the creation of Special Snowflake Syndrome. I am not alone in feeling that social media (for all its positives) definitely poses risks. Social media, by emphasizing the superficial, focusing on the physical, and creating the expectation of instant gratification and look-at-me 24-7, has contributed to a "powder keg because of the amount of stress young people have to live with" (Buckland, 2016, para 5). This obsession with the above results in and reinforces many of the symptoms of Special Snowflake Syndrome.

In addition to the emotional distress created by obsessions with unrealistic appearances, success, and celebrity that most people will not obtain, we see the distress manifest in our everyday lives. Dr. Gene Beresin, in a recent article, stated that "50-60% of college students have a psychiatric disorder" (Marshall, 2016, para 2). It is beyond frightening to imagine that number of college students experiencing such a degree of distress that they meet criteria for a diagnosable mental health condition. Dr. Beresin also added that "a college student kills himself every day" (2016, para 7).

My clinical opinion is that at least some portion of the above is due to special snowflake traits and full-blown Special Snowflake Syndrome. Consider the signs and symptoms of the disorder and it makes perfect sense: A person demands special treatment due to a sense of entitlement and elevation of their needs above others. They are easily offended by others' words and behaviors, in part because they are unable to consider that other opinions have validity. They then display childish, even temper tantrum-type responses when thwarted or disagreed with. And at the end of the day, believe others are the problem.

How is that person going to function in the world? Part of my proposed personality disorder is the prediction that they can't. This is reflected in the dangerous consequences detailed above: 50-60% of college students with a diagnosable mental health disorder and one college student per day taking their own life.

The Tragedy of Microaggressions

If you are unfamiliar with the term, dictionary.com (n.d., para 1) defines a microaggression as "a subtle but offensive comment or action directed at a minority or other nondominant group that is often unintentional or unconsciously reinforces a stereotype". That seems pretty clear. Or is it?

According to Dr. Derald Sue, a professor of psychology at Columbia University, "microaggressions are inherently ambiguous" and it's probably best to believe the person declaring something a microaggression (Torres, 2014).

Uh-oh. Now we're going to have a problem. All a person has to do is **label** something a microaggression – by definition something offensive – and they are *automatically* accurate. Is it any wonder so many of the claims of microaggressions are coming from hypersensitive individuals?

Obviously, -isms still exist in our culture (whether racism, sexism, ageism, etc) BUT when people are increasingly displaying Special Snowflake Syndrome traits, this starts to look like more and more people chronically offended, completely caught up in playing the victim, and unable to engage in real dialogue about concerns. It goes back to…agree with me or you're wrong.

Remember my example from last chapter of the college students who declared inaccurate ethnic cafeteria food was "insensitive", "culturally inappropriate", "ridiculous", and "disrespectful" (Licea & Italiano, 2015, paras 1, 5 and 6)? What I didn't mention then was that the students **also** declared that such imperfect cooking was an example of a microaggression.

The other tragedy of microaggressions then is that while we're so busy having to fight questionable charges of an -ism, like above, we ignore real aggression, like school buses used by Jewish students being set on fire in Brooklyn (Shallwani and MacMillan, 2016) or a gay couple in Atlanta having boiling water poured on them while they slept (Richardson, 2016).

Educating someone if they say something blatantly racist, sexist, homophobic, etc, is up to the individual hearing the words. We have gone so far beyond that it has become "divisive hypersensitivity, in which casual remarks are blown out of proportion" and, to quote Harry Stein (in Vega, 2014, para 18), contributing editor to City Journal, "the impulse to exaggerate the meaning of such encounters in the interest of perpetually seeing oneself as a victim" is the result.

Tyranny of Safe Spaces

Beyond the microaggression controversy, there are "safe spaces" and "safe space screamers". A safe space is a place where nothing anyone can remotely ever find offensive is allowed. It's the haven that the hypersensitive individuals with Special Snowflake Syndrome need in order to feel secure. Unfortunately, these are usually located on college campuses, though not always; a recent article described celebrity safe spaces, where they can now filter out any negative commentary about themselves on Twitter (Kew, 2016).

Have you heard of Milo Yiannopoulos? He's a journalist and editor with Breitbart News, an online website; love him or hate him, he's an extremely outspoken conservative lightning rod. He frequently appears at college events discussing his conservative and polarizing views on topics ranging from feminism to Islam.

Just about any Milo event brings with it protesters; one event at DePaul University was disrupted by students (who apparently don't understand free speech or comedy). But, the most appalling result of this event was the Women's Studies Department creating a safe space for all the fragile snowflakes who were "profoundly disturbed and distressed by the deep harm and damage" caused by Milo's mere presence (Hadfield, 2016, para 2).

Or how about the group therapy session held at Rutgers University after a Milo appearance? Or University of Pittsburgh Student Government Board members discussing the "traumatized" students (Nash, 2016, para 4) and feeling "hurt" (University of Pittsburgh, Student Government Board Statement, 2016, para 1) after a Milo appearance? I could go on, but you get the point.

A safe space screamer on the other hand is, according to urbandictionary.com (2016, para 1), "a person who uses intimidation, accusations, threats and/or shouting in order to prevent others from saying or doing something they find offensive. These people exercise their own right to free speech in order to limit the free speech of those with whom they disagree."

An individual with Special Snowflake Syndrome is much more likely to want offense-free zones, due to their hyper-sensitivity, but then are quite likely to overreact when outside those spaces (or if someone does not "respect" the safe space) and become a safe space screamer. An example of this comes courtesy of an assistant professor at another university who not only denied a reporter access to public property on the university, but actually is heard on video demanding the reporter leave and even calling for others to help forcibly remove him from the space (Moyer, Miller, & Holley, 2015).

"Why shouldn't I have it my way?"

A particular challenging aspect of the individual consequences of Special Snowflake Syndrome arises from two facts: there does still exist bigotry and discrimination, and it's human nature to want to do things our own way. How do I find the balance? The easiest way to consider this is to ask the question, "What happens when what you want comes up against what I want?" Can we both be right? I'll address this therapeutically in Part II of the book. Right now, I want to look at the individual consequence of always believing you're entitled to have things your way.

The fact is, if somebody says something inappropriate to me, it may be perfectly appropriate for me to respond and let them know that. It also may be perfectly appropriate for me to ask for what I want. However, the individual consequence of the narcissism, hypersensitivity, and over-reactivity of Special Snowflake Syndrome means that the person will simply not be capable of recognizing that it also can be **just as** reasonable for someone else to get their way, or that what someone said or did was **not** actually offensive or inappropriate.

The bottom line for the individual with Special Snowflake Syndrome is that psychologically when they elevate their needs above others, are unable to see another's perspective, display child-like behavior including temper tantrums or narcissistic rage, demand special treatment, have a sense of entitlement, and believe everyone else is the problem, they will be unable to look inward at their roles and responsibilities in their own life as well as the larger society, will be stuck in a perpetual state of being a victim, and will experience constant dissatisfaction with their own life as well as their functioning in society.

Dangerous Societal Consequences

As I wrote at the end of the last chapter and under this chapter's **Dangerous Individual Consequences** section, we are becoming a completely self-absorbed, fragile, whining population. What does this mean for the future of society?

There are three dangerous sociological consequences of the proliferation of Special Snowflake Syndrome on society. It may not be immediately obvious why each of these is a problem, perhaps because we can point to times when it has not been. As you continue reading, you'll see exactly why, when they become extensions of an individual's Special Snowflake Syndrome, they are HUGE problems.

First, we look for and align ourselves with others who agree with us on at least one major point.

Second, we then look for institutions to agree with us and drive out those who disagree.

Third, as a society, we begin to sow extreme divisiveness and discontent between the people who disagree.

Aligning with Like-Minded Individuals

Regardless of whether an individual has Special Snowflake Syndrome or not, it is practically hard-wired into all humans to have a need for belonging. Obviously, aligning with like-minded individuals can be extremely beneficial to us on every level. I can join a group of fellow writers, a running club, or a small business association to meet my intangible need to belong, along with other more tangible benefits, like critiques of my writing, safety of running with a buddy, and marketing ideas from my group members.

I would go a step further and posit, though, that part of the reason we want to band with others is that we want agreement and validation of our beliefs. This also is not usually a bad thing. When individuals with Special Snowflake Syndrome decide to align with like-minded individuals, however, negative events typically transpire.

Think about the concept of the social justice warrior. Once a compliment, this now-derisive phrase typically refers to the perception that someone is overreacting to something they have deemed offensive (Ohlheiser, 2015). This is relevant to the sociological impact of Special Snowflake Syndrome because much of this overreaction takes place online, where the **warriors** seek out others who agree with them.

In the first week of July 2016, we saw an interesting example of overreaction of folks coupled with aligning with like-minded individuals. Dueling Jesse Williams' petitions! In a cnn.com article, you can read the incredible details (France, 2016). This story began when Mr. Williams (an actor) gave a speech at an event; a bunch of people got offended and demanded he be fired, via online petition (of course). Then, a bunch of other people, offended by those taking offense, created their OWN petition in support of Mr. Williams. All of these folks, per usual, are missing the point. Where's the real dialogue about the content of the speech? And, truly, what impact did any of this have on them?

Earlier I mentioned Milo Yiannopoulos. Perhaps you're one of the individuals who doesn't particularly like his brand of activism, so you maybe have sympathy for negative campus reactions to him. What about Condoleeza Rice? Or Sean "Diddy" Combs? Or Barbara Bush? Or Barack Obama, Colin Powell, or Michael Bloomberg? Or one of the 148 potential commencement speakers since 1987 who have been protested against by students, resulting in 39 cancellations (Frumin, 2014)?

Typically, a small but very vocal minority expresses their displeasure with a speaker's opposing views and/or past actions; if the speaker cancels or gets booed off stage, we see the negative consequences of special snowflakes aligning. At this stage, though, they haven't yet moved onto bigger things.

Aligning with like-minded individuals becomes problematic when the narcissistic special snowflakes feel emboldened by the support and agreement of others, and thus decide that everyone needs to support and agree with them. And that's when we move into the second step. Individuals with Special Snowflake Syndrome, now banded together around at least one issue on which they agree, look for institutions to help them drive out those who disagree.

Institutions as Weapons

Once groups of individuals with Special Snowflake Syndrome get together, they of course ask various institutions to reflect their beliefs. Often this results in anybody who disagrees with them being shut down, ostracized, or even fired. Here are just a few examples:

How about the story of a Marquette University professor who was suspended and threatened with firing for daring to blog about a fellow academic who reportedly told a student that his conservative views would "not be tolerated" in her class (Ruse, 2016, para 1)? The special snowflakes were able to convince the school to toe their line.

Or how about the Yale University lecturer who was let go for daring to suggest that adult college students are capable of choosing their own Halloween costumes? This was considered offensive. I encourage you to watch the video at https://www.thefire.org/yale-students-demand-resignations-from-faculty-members-over-halloween-email/ where yet another college student talks about a safe space where no dissenting opinions exist (TheFire.org, 2015). A young woman at about 2:30 in the video states she will leave if the lecturer's husband doesn't issue the demanded apology. In the second video, a young woman literally screams at him when he calmly says he does not agree with her. Again, we see the special snowflakes' ability to create institutional divide that results in actual job loss for someone who disagreed with them.

Sometimes, the special snowflakes aren't aiming at a specific person, but at a specific population. They still can endeavor to get institutional support to exert power over others in an attempt to force agreement on challenging issues. For example, a committee of students and faculty at Oregon State University, in a well-meaning effort to reduce "injustice", have proposed a five course online course on social justice for new students (Nardi, 2016, para 10). Similar to other universities, and along with their Bias Response Team, this seems yet another attempt by an institution to indoctrinate students to think a certain way, and as one dissenter commented in the article, "They are being trained — not taught, but trained — to think everything that offends them is a bias incident" (2016, para 16).

Just so nobody gets the sense that this is an issue only for college students (though they certainly get a lot of press!), here's one from Australia. The Fair Workplace Commission, an Australian tribunal, determined that a woman bullied her co-worker by 'unfriending' her on Facebook (Pearlman, 2015). To be fair to the tribunal, technically they stated there was a pattern that in their opinion constituted workplace bullying. But, still. Facebook unfriending was mentioned as an example and the issue originated with a special snowflake who dragged an institutional tribunal into the matter. And they agreed.

What do all of the above have in common? The Special Snowflake Syndrome belief of, **Agree with me or be vilified**, followed by institutional support of this divisiveness. What this leads to is increasing population discontent.

Animosity and Antagonism

Because we focus on our differences instead of our commonalities, we sow more and more population discontent. We don't ever want to hear anything negative about ourselves, our groups, our families. This includes anything that we simply disagree with. Note that I am not saying it's okay to emotionally abuse someone, but here's the thing. The ridiculous level of insecurity that exists for an individual with Special Snowflake Syndrome results in **any** disagreement perceived as abusiveness. The divide between groups that disagree becomes wider and wider, and true discourse between them becomes nearly impossible.

When is the last time you heard folks on opposite sides of polarizing issues, like guns or abortion, have a reasoned debate? Do I hear crickets? Exactly. Few people seem able to speak rationally with those who disagree with them and it is my opinion that this is a societal result of the increasing numbers of individuals with Special Snowflake Syndrome.

Interestingly, this attempt to eliminate all disagreement and negativity typically results in the exact opposite outcome. In becoming upset over everything, demanding others fall in line, and yelling when that doesn't happen, what we've seen is increasing projection of negativity within our culture, and it's most obviously reflected in our pop culture. In a world of instant gratification and social media, it's become easier and easier to immediately express one's negative opinion about anything and everything, creating artificial divides (e.g., Marvel versus DC comic movie rivalry) that may result in very real pain and consequences (Truitt, 2016).

Even well-meaning attempts to help close the gap often result in inadvertently widening it. The Office of Arts and Culture of Seattle, Washington, currently offers a class on White Fragility, defined by them as "the inability of white people to tolerate racial stress" (Quinn, 2016, para 4). Despite the obvious intent to improve understanding and communication, the likelihood of this class doing anything but sow additional population disconnect is made crystal clear by the comments under the article. And how could it not? Instead of focusing on how to improve communication on tough issues, it still largely is looking to assign blame.

Even more unfortunate is that as societal consequences continue to increase, this will also continue to spill over into negative political consequences.

Dangerous Political Consequences

Three dangerous political consequences follow from the above progression of individuals with Special Snowflake Syndrome coming together to create institutional divisiveness. The first is the ease with which we describe those that disagree with us in harsher and harsher terms. The second is the progression to actually suing others for (in the loosest sense of the word) wronging us. The third is that we actually create (or desire to create) regulations, rules, and laws restricting the freedom of others.

Name-Calling and Trash Talking

Regarding the first political result: it is much easier to describe the "other" as wrong and evil, so that we are therefore right and good. And as far as I can see, no groups are exempt. Have you ever heard a Republican describe a Democrat as a socialist libtard who wants us to live in a nanny state, or a Democrat describe a Republican as a racist misogynist who values guns over lives? Of course you have. Although the parties have always had division of varying degrees, a Pew Research Center report found, "Americans are more ideologically polarized today than they've been in at least two decades. Their representatives in Congress are divided too" (DeSilver, 2014, para 1).

What about within the parties? To use one example (from my home state), in May 2016, the divisiveness within the Democratic party moved beyond name-calling to the disaster that was the Nevada Democratic

Convention. Reading the completely contradictory descriptions from Hillary-supporters versus Bernie-supporters, even from people who **were there**, shows the incredible divisiveness.

For more name-calling, and even indirectly implying someone doesn't exist, let's look at the fitness mom controversies on social media. Probably the most well known is Maria Kang, who posted a picture of herself looking quite fit, along with her three young children, under the caption, 'What's your excuse?' Believing her intention to motivate others would be clear, she was nevertheless almost instantly reviled and accused of shaming other mothers who were not as fit as her (Murphy, 2013). Her response asked them to "own the thoughts that come out of your own head [or] get used to hating many other things for the rest of your life" (para 11). Kang wasn't referring to individuals with Special Snowflake Syndrome, but likely there were some in her audience.

All of this begs the question: how does this woman's state of being impact anybody else? How is this so offensive that other women actually respond by saying women like her are not "real" women? Of course they are. And the individuals making the comments, in their zeal to be offended, likely don't even begin to realize how invalidating such comments are.

Legal Attacks

When individuals with Special Snowflake Syndrome become enraged, one consequence may be an increasing amount of litigation. Think of people who have sued because their coffee was too hot (Peterson, 2014), there was too much ice in their drink (McLean, 2016), or the dry cleaners lost their pants (Myall, 2014).

A case currently in the **federal** court system started as a fight between two sorority sisters at Penn State University (Roebuck, 2016). In the case, one sorority sister filed a defamation and breach-of-contract against the other sorority sister's parents and the school itself. As the writer pens in the article, this "spat" that normally would have been likely "dismissed as a typical drama between young women" (that also involves a bit of helicopter parenting) has instead become an actual federal court case (2016, para 3).

In July 2016, a professor at one university actually filed a civil rights complaint against **another** university for having a 'women-only' study lounge (Owens, 2016). He filed the complaint, stating, in essence, that its existence was a Title IX (federal law) violation. I'm no Title IX scholar, so I won't debate the legalities. I will, however, give my opinion that this guy may be a special snowflake. How does this impact him? Why does he care? Whose cause is he championing?

Now, admittedly, some of the people with their ridiculous frivolous lawsuits may just be greedy, or have some other unknown motivator. But, I suspect that over time, we will see more and more special snowflakes go the avenue of increased litigation to settle their grievances. It will move from, **you will agree with me or I'll vilify you**, to **you will agree with me or I'll sue you**.

Restricting Freedom

What's even scarier than the name-calling and disruption is when this actually moves into changing rules, regulations, and laws. As a result of the societal consequences of Special Snowflake Syndrome detailed above, we restrict freedom in an effort to quiet the increasingly loud clamoring of every special interest group under the sun. These can range from unofficial, to implied, to codified.

Unofficial censorship exists when someone's comments bring a hail of backlash, usually indicating how and why the person failed to toe the line, effectively silencing that person. Under negative political consequences, we blur the line between unofficial and official censorship. Think of 'trigger warnings' on books and college courses. In an August 2014 report, the American Association of University Professors discussed concerns of the chilling effect of such warnings and the expectation that many relevant material sources would be removed due to their "triggering" nature. The report explicitly states, "The presumption that students need to be protected rather than challenged in a classroom is at once infantilizing and anti-intellectual" (para 3). When you have special snowflakes doing the dictating, this is an unsurprising result.

Consider too the multitude of university responses to the demands of special snowflakes:

At the University of North Carolina at Chapel Hill, in an effort to minimize microaggressions, released employee guidelines warning employees to beware of everything from complimenting women on their shoes (since this would apparently indicate valuing her appearance over her intellect) to not inviting colleagues for a round of golf (because it assumes the person can afford an expensive sport) (Starnes, 2016).

At Princeton University, a four-page memo lays out exactly how they can be more inclusive – by essentially eliminating the word 'man' (Beaman, 2016). To a degree, this makes sense; saying partner or spouse, instead of man and wife. But, when it starts to dictate things like saying 'artificial' instead of 'manmade', then perhaps it's time to consider that the line of common sense has been crossed.

Marquette University's Writing Center wrote a language policy implying that students could face negative consequences by failing to use gender-neutral language (Beaman, 2016). Again, the intention may be positive, but dictating language and implying negative consequences for failing to fall in line with those dictates crosses a line.

Here's one that's silly on the surface, but amounts to the same thing. Throwing food away in Seattle is now outlawed. Failing to compost such waste will now be subject to a fine. Putting aside the debate of the merits of recycling, do we really want people rooting through our trash? Also, the city is essentially stating, we don't trust you to make your own decisions, so we're telling you what to do. Peering into our garbage cans seems over the top.

And, finally, a bit of a hot button topic, but what about hate speech legislation? On the surface, this may seem like a fine idea. According to dictionary.com (n.d., para 1), hate speech is "speech that attacks, threatens, or insults a person or group on the basis of national origin, ethnicity, color, religion, gender, gender identity, sexual orientation, or disability". But much like with microaggressions, the label gets applied to broader and broader comments until, as the Washington Times described, it becomes "an incoherent concept that confuses more than it clarifies" (Nossel, 2016).

Individuals with Special Snowflake Syndrome can have a field day declaring everything they find offensive to be hate speech. Within international law, hate speech consists of ideas like inciting genocide (article19.org, n.d.). This makes sense. Thus far, laws have been limited to, for example, restrictions on speech that creates a hostile work environment (which is not technically considered hate speech legislation; see Volokh, 2015). There have not been fundamental changes to the First Amendment guaranteeing free speech. With enough noise and moving from the unofficial censorship described earlier, it's a natural next step for the special snowflakes to want and scream for official censorship.

Now that I've established *why* Special Snowflake Syndrome has dangerous far-reaching negative consequences for individuals and society, the second part of this book will focus on curing this Syndrome. Throughout, I'll continue to use these ripped-from-the-headlines examples of the Syndrome. Read on to learn how we can cure Special Snowflake Syndrome in three (not easy, but doable) steps.

If you identified with Special Snowflake Syndrome yourself, or even just some of the criteria, consider how to apply the next sections to your own thoughts and interactions.

If you didn't identify with Special Snowflake Syndrome, but you know people who behave this way, try to help them see the challenges in their flawed logic and to experiment with the following recommendations.

Good luck!

Chapter Three Summary

Individual psychological dangers of Special Snowflake Syndrome creating a nation of victims include poor mental health and suicide, the tragedy of microaggressions, tyranny of safe spaces, and challenges of not always having their way.

Societal dangers of Special Snowflake Syndrome include individuals with the Syndrome aligning with others who agree that something is offensive, using institutions as weapons to drive out disagreements, and creating antagonism and animosity by sowing extreme divisiveness and discontent within the population from the disagreement.

Political dangers of the proliferation of Special Snowflake Syndrome from individuals through institutions results in name-calling and trash-talking, legal attacks, and actual creation/changing of rules, regulations, and laws to restrict the freedom of others.

Notes

PART II

CURING

SPECIAL
SNOWFLAKE
SYNDROME

4 ASSUME BENEVOLENCE

You've undoubtedly heard the expression, 'To assume makes an ass out of you and me'. The basis of this expression likely has its roots in the idea that assumptions are made despite a lack of concrete evidence. For an official definition: according to dictionary.com (n.d., para 1), to assume is "to take for granted, or without proof".

In addition, typically assumptions are negative and involve predicting the future and/or believing we can read another's mind. Would it surprise you to learn that a type of positive assumption forms the first technique in saving the world from Special Snowflake Syndrome?

Assuming benevolence also comes from a place of incomplete evidence for the motivations of others; the key difference is that we're choosing to assume **benevolence**. What does that mean? Again from dictionary.com (n.d., para 1), benevolence is "desire to do good to others" or "an act of kindness".

So what does **assuming benevolence** mean? It means that in the absence of any evidence, we are choosing to believe that someone's words or behavior were motivated by the desire to be kind. Or at the very least, we're giving someone the benefit of the doubt, choosing to believe neutral motivation.

Wow, that's heady stuff, right? And the complete opposite of what someone with Special Snowflake Syndrome does. That's why it's our first step in curing the world of Special Snowflake Syndrome. Instead of seeing everything we don't like as offensive, wrong, or bad, we choose to assume benevolence.

If you're having a hard time seeing the application of that, let's look at exactly how we can apply it to each of the eight signs or criteria of Special Snowflake Syndrome, using both new examples and some of the examples from Chapter 2...

Frequent demanding of special treatment regardless of circumstances.

This criterion often reflects two related ideas: the special snowflake belief that rules apply to others and the special snowflake belief that they deserve more (different or better) than others. Let's apply the cure of assuming benevolence to the special snowflake sign of demanding special treatment using our university example from Chapter 2:

A group of students at Yale University in a program of study for an English major, demanded the special treatment of being excused from two required courses that they found offensive because of the lack of representation by women, people of color, and gays (Campbell, 2016).

How might these students use the cure of assuming benevolence to manage their demand for special treatment? They can start by asking themselves:

> For what purpose is the university requiring the classes?

If the students are honest with themselves, they will be able to recognize that the university requires two classes in "Major English Poets" because for a program of study leading to the degree of English, it is logical to study the leading figures in that area.

It's possible the students may respond, "those are the only the most well-known poets because the women, people of color, and gays were either not allowed to produce similar works or were/are ignored because they were not white men". Remember Special Snowflake

Syndrome sign #5 of being easily offended, especially when triggered by perceived injustice. It's possible the students would initially dig their heals in because of this. We can still apply the technique of assuming benevolence by then asking:

Were the faculty around back then and are they choosing these poets to keep other-than-white-men down today?

If the students are honest with themselves, they will acknowledge that the faculty are asking them to study these poets, not to oppress, but to educate, and that if one is to say they have studied English literature, then in the interests of completeness, these poets naturally would be included. [And remember, the students can always problem solve and work with the faculty to develop/encourage, if they don't already exist, additional classes that include the groups of authors they would like to see recognized.]

If individuals with Special Snowflake Syndrome can assume benevolent reasons behind what is offered (or not) to them from others in social, relationship, and work/education situations, they would be able to learn to curb the demand for special treatment in all those situations.

Sense of entitlement or unrealistic expectation of favorable treatment from others regardless of deservedness.

We probably all know that person who thinks the world ought to be handed to him or her on a silver platter. They believe hard work isn't necessary because they are so special and entitled to success that it will just naturally be given to them. Possibly you are or know that person? Let's look at a recent example of the special snowflake symptom of a **sense of entitlement** and note two things: who do you agree with in the scenario and can you identify how we will apply the cure of assuming benevolence to counteract the belief?

In mid-June 2016, a fascinating Dear Abby advice column posted online (Van Buren, 2016). An individual, not identified as male or female, wrote in asking for advice. Chris, we'll call this person, expressed the entitled expectation that their parents would co-sign for a loan to attend law school and appeared genuinely baffled that the parents declined to co-sign the loan.

There are two pieces of evidence of entitlement in this scenario. The first is the expectation that because Chris asked the parents for assistance that answer would automatically be yes. What clinches this as obvious entitlement is that Chris also writes in the letter, "it surprises me that it doesn't embarrass them that I may have to ask another family member for help" (Van Buren, 2016, para 3). Oh my goodness! By now, you hopefully clearly see the entitlement in this example. Chris could look at applying the cure of assuming benevolence by asking:

> Am I **entitled** to this assistance or is it just **preference**?

What is meant by the above question? Part of assuming benevolence when considering the belief that one is entitled to something is asking ourselves **why** we believe the way that we do. In this scenario, is it simply because Chris developed the expectation that parents contribute to college for their children? Or is it a broader expectation that simply because Chris would **prefer** the financial assistance therefore it is a guarantee? If we're honest and recognize that it's just preference – because everybody is perfectly able to provide or not provide requested assistance – then we can take the second step of assuming benevolence for the reasons why the request was rejected.

In this scenario, to push pause on the sense of entitlement, Chris can first recognize that nobody is required to provide assistance simply because it was requested. Chris then can consider that the parents said no for any number of reasons, many of which possibly weren't even related to Chris (e.g., maybe they're experiencing financial challenges right now and co-signing on any loan would not be justified).

Assuming benevolence to cure a sense of entitlement is recognizing both that nobody owes us anything and that the reasons people may not provide what we want may have one of many possibly explanations, so why not select a neutral or even positive one?

Elevation of their needs above others, regardless of the objective importance of those needs, or the impact on others.

If my needs are more important than yours, anytime you don't do what I want, I'm going to become upset. In addition, I'm going to take actions that benefit me, without regard to the impact on you. The individual with Special Snowflake Syndrome is unable to give the other person even the minimum of the benefit of the doubt, or consider the impact of their own behavior on the other person, because to the individual with Special Snowflake Syndrome it simply doesn't matter. All that matters are their own needs, as we can revisit in this example from Chapter 2:

University students objected to the ways in which specific ethnic food was made for them, and in fact actually described it as offensive for a number of reasons (Soave, 2015; Licea & Italiano, 2015). Although I used this in Chapter 2 as an example of a **sense of entitlement and unrealistic expectations**, it also fits here as an **elevation of their needs, regardless of importance or impact on others**.

The university students in this example can use the technique of assuming benevolence to reduce their distress at their elevated and comparatively unimportant needs regarding the exact nature of food being prepared by asking themselves:

For what purpose were the cafeteria staff making the ethnic food?

This one is actually a relatively easy application of assuming benevolence. If the students are honest with themselves, they will recognize that the ethnic food was being prepared to offer variety to the students. They can choose to assume that the offering of additional food choices was meant as something **nice**. By assuming that the workers were actually trying to do something nice, they can reduce the level of distress they are creating for themselves over an objectively unimportant need.

Secondarily, as I wrote in chapter 2: How could the students expect that the cafeteria workers would know exactly how to make every single dish exactly the way it would have been made in the students' **interpretation** of their various culture? [In the interests of problem solving, if they would like the food prepared differently, instead of overreacting and considering the current preparation as something offensive, another option could have been to simply state that they have suggestions for improving the offerings to the benefit of all.]

Inability to recognize the perspectives of others, or that the opinions of others may have validity.

Remember what I said in Part I about how this symptom of Special Snowflake Syndrome is the flip side of **elevating your needs above others**? Often people <u>do</u> elevate their needs above others because they are unable to see the other person's perspective (and this idea is so important to curing Special Snowflake Syndrome that it has its own chapter next in the book!) Let's apply assuming benevolence to my example from Chapter 2:

An associate professor of political science wrote an opinion piece stating her decision to not present the presidential candidates equally because she believed to do so would be dishonest (Ianello, 2016). This clearly demonstrates her inability to see that the opinions of others have validity, since it is unlikely that every single student in her classes supports the same candidate as her.

The professor can apply assuming benevolence by considering the reasons others might disagree with her in class. Instead of her current negative assumption that balanced discourse is dishonest, she can ask herself:

What are the perspectives of those in class who disagree?

Right now, the inference is that if a student disagrees with her stated positions, that student is just wrong. An assistant professor's role is to educate and encourage thinking, even if it goes in a different direction than one's own. Although one can also assume benevolence for the professor's position (she's doing what she believes is morally justified), it's important for her to consider why the members of her class may disagree and that they may be disagreeing because they honestly do not agree with her. Just about any time a person feels the need to justify their behavior, they probably ought not to engage in the behavior.

Remember the key with taking the other person's perspective when it comes to assuming benevolence is that one does not have evidence one way or the another, so one consciously chooses an explanation that gives the other person the benefit of the doubt. This does two things: helps someone to calm down and reinforces considering other people. Something that individuals with Special Snowflake Syndrome often struggle to do.

Easily offended by others' words and behaviors, especially if triggered by perceived injustice.

One of the biggest "triggers" for the individual with Special Snowflake Syndrome is without question the "offensive" comment or behavior. Of course, they consider so many things offensive, it may be hard to keep track. Let's use an example from the news to practice assuming benevolence with regard to the Special Snowflake Syndrome sign of being easily offended by others.

In summer 2016, two battling hashtags took center stage – #blacklivesmatter versus #alllivesmatter. Largely waged on social media (where these almost always seem to occur), a subset of folks on both "sides" demonstrated the special snowflake sign of **being easily offended**. On the one side, you had folks who believed that every single person who typed #alllivesmatter was a racist who doesn't care about black people. On the other side, you had folks who believed that every single person who typed #blacklivesmatter was a militant domestic terrorist intent on killing police officers. For those who found themselves on either side of these extreme beliefs, offended by the other side's hashtag…ask yourself:

For what purpose did the other "side" write their hashtag?

Assuming benevolence involves taking a neutral or positive stance in terms of the reasons for the comment or behavior that one finds offensive. By giving the other person the benefit of the doubt, one can calm down and perhaps even have a rational conversation. What would that look like?

The #alllivesmatter folks can recognize that the motivation behind the #blacklivesmatter movement is fear of harm and a desire for safe, respectful interactions within society. They can remind themselves that the purpose of the hashtag is to raise awareness and that the vast majority of folks typing that are not militant terrorists wanting to kill police officers and/or all white people.

The #blacklivesmatter folks can recognize that motivation behind the #alllivesmatter movement is fear of destabilizing society and a desire for safe, respectful interactions within society. They can remind themselves that the purpose of the hashtag is an attempt to reduce what is viewed as unhelpful divisiveness and that the purpose is not a racist notion dismissing the concerns of black people.

Did you notice the motivations are largely similar? When we assume benevolence and give the other side the benefit of the doubt, often what we find is that we share common ground and we're offended for no real reason (I'll talk more about this in the next chapter on **Taking Others' Perspectives**).

Displaying developmentally inappropriate behavior in response to perceived disagreeable actions of others.

A hallmark of what we witness with an individual with Special Snowflake Syndrome is the sign of developmentally inappropriate, or child-like, behavior… although childish would probably be a better descriptor! Let's look at the application of assumed benevolence with this example from Chapter 2:

People of all ideologies are posting non-stop political posts on social media, declaring dire predictions if particular presidential candidates win, and stating they are moving to Canada if their preferred candidate does not win (Carroll, 2016).

Although I know this sounds silly, but seriously declaring you're moving to Canada (or any other location outside the United States) if your preferred presidential candidate does not win, is a developmentally inappropriate response to the perceived disagreeable actions of others.

This is an interesting example to work with because the application may not seem that obvious. Who exactly is the person supposed to assume the benevolence of? Let's apply the technique of assuming benevolence to this scenario by asking ourselves:

For what reason are the candidates running for office?

Putting aside the cynical reactions many people might have to this question (e.g., power, money, fame), let's take a step back and answer the question with neutral or positive eyes. The individuals declaring they're moving out of the country if their candidate doesn't win can assume the benevolence of the candidates. Specifically, the candidate who is **not** getting their vote.

If one can assume a benevolent reason behind a candidate running for president – such as wanting to make the world a better place – then perhaps one can also then realize that having a childish reaction of 'taking my ball and going home' is an irrational response. If one chooses to assume both candidates are running for office for positive reasons, then one can look at the election of either as having positive potential.

If someone finds they are unable to do this, they may want to consider the source of such animosity and consider that maybe they are the overreacting special snowflake.

Inappropriate and/or intense displays of anger, often in the form of a narcissistic rage.

This next sign of Special Snowflake Syndrome is the extreme version of the prior symptom of **displaying**

developmentally inappropriate behavior. What this typically looks like is someone who expresses themselves in a childish manner initially, they do not receive the response they're looking for, and then it devolves into a full blown temper tantrum.

I also call this narcissistic rage for two reasons. Narcissists almost by definition will meet some of my criteria for Special Snowflake Syndrome because of their similar beliefs they are unique, special, and entitled. Rage is added because by the time the special snowflake has lost control, the emotional component has grown far beyond simple anger and has become out of control rage.

Remember the Yale University lecturer and her husband I mentioned earlier? She wrote an email essentially stating that college students were capable of selecting their Halloween costumes without being dictated to by the university about what was appropriate (Friedersdorf, 2015). The response by some in the university community was swift and fiercely negative. There were immediate calls for the resignation of both the woman and her husband. There were ridiculous numbers of hyperbolic statements about how the students could no longer feel safe on campus.

The couple chose to meet with concerned students in a public forum on campus. Check out the video on YouTube (TheFire.org, 2015) and note the point at which the woman speaking to the husband descends into a narcissistic rage. Again, she literally screams at him and makes statements that unless he completely agrees with her, and concedes he and his wife are completely in the wrong, there's no point in even speaking to the couple.

Crystal clear example of the Special Snowflake Syndrome sign of the temper tantrum. How can we use the Special Snowflake Syndrome cure of assumed benevolence to eliminate the temper tantrum example of narcissistic rage?

Honestly, it's going to be pretty hard to use any skills in the moment when they're in a full blown temper tantrum. Think about a child; are they receptive to making changes in the moment? Nah. We wait for them to tire themselves out. And then we try to help them make changes! The same goes for the special snowflake adult. Ideally, you'll catch the behavior and make changes while it's still just childish behavior and not a tantrum yet.

If we miss that window, we can apply assuming benevolence after the fact, once they've calmed down, by considering the perspectives of others and specifically considering alternative explanations for the initial email. In this instance, one can easily identify that the lecturer wrote the email to empower college students to believe they are more capable than many of them seem to think they are. With some perspective taking, one can see she had quite good intentions, in fact, whether or not one agrees with her.

Believes others are the sole source of any problem, negative emotion, or poor outcome.

As first expressed under the **Psychological Features** of Special Snowflake Syndrome chapter, this final sign is the most insidious and difficult to address. How does that complicate applying **assumed benevolence** to curing the problem? By applying assumed benevolence to the earlier signs, you've seen how we are considering an assumption (without any evidence) of benevolence (good or at least neutral motivations). If an individual with Special Snowflake Syndrome believes everyone else is the problem, it's going to be a hard sell to get them to consider positive, or even just neutral, motivations in others.

Let's apply the technique to the example from Chapter 2 of the "Are you beach-body ready?" billboard:

A woman sees a billboard with a fit woman in a bikini staring back at her, the words, "Are you beach-body ready?" emblazoned upon it. Offended by this billboard, she creates a petition, demanding the billboard be removed, which many other people sign (Crocker, 2015).

The woman in the scenario, as well as the individuals who signed the petition, are assigning responsibility for their own thoughts and emotions to the creators of the billboard for their **choice** to both interpret the billboard as fat-shaming and to feel negative about it and themselves as a result.

This hypersensitivity and the resulting distress can be reduced by the offended individuals asking themselves the following question:

For what reason did the company display the billboard?

Remember with **assuming benevolence**, we do not have evidence one way or the other. Is it likely that the marketing company, the public relations firm, and the product company itself were all intending to fat-shame and insult women? Of course not! How on earth would that sell their product?

A completely reasonable benevolent assumption is that the companies involved in the display of the billboard were attempting to motivate and encourage individuals who want to get into a specific shape to try their product (and there have been similar billboards and outcries for companies selling everything from gym memberships to plastic surgery to nutritional supplements).

A consequence of the individual with Special Snowflake Syndrome believing others are the sole source of any problem, negative emotion, or poor outcome is that in situations like this, the overreaction to something that in fact has no bearing on their lives, results in stagnation. When assuming benevolence, in addition to choosing to see that no offense was meant, by removing artificial negative reasons for lack of success, the individual with Special Snowflake Syndrome can actually be the success they already believe they should be.

Assuming benevolence is an amazingly powerful technique to help a person (with or without full Special Snowflake Syndrome) begin the process of recognizing that all people are of value, one person's needs do not necessarily supersede others, and that in considering neutral or even positive motivations of others, the individual with special snowflake tendencies can reduce levels of distress and start highly productive conversations, even about the most contentious of topics.

Assuming benevolence is only the first step however. In the next chapter, I'll expound on the importance of taking other people's perspectives, a natural follow-on to assuming benevolence, and its role in reducing and/or eliminating the signs of Special Snowflake Syndrome.

Chapter Four Summary

Chapter 4 introduced the first step in curing Special Snowflake Syndrome: assuming benevolence. This means that in the absence of any evidence, we choose to believe that someone's words or behavior were motivated by the desire to be kind. Or at the very least, we give someone the benefit of the doubt, choosing to believe neutral motivation.

In order to do this, whether we are the individual with Special Snowflake Syndrome, or we are interacting with someone with the Syndrome, we ask ourselves, or ask them to consider:

What is a possible neutral or positive motivation for the other person's comment or behavior?

Then we choose, or encourage the individual with Special Snowflake Syndrome to choose, to believe that alternative neutral or positive explanation.

Notes

5 TAKE OTHERS' PERSPECTIVES

When you read the following, what comes to mind?

"When everybody is special, nobody is special"

It is literally impossible to satisfy all of the people all of the time. Most folks know this to be true, so they focus on what's important to them and their larger community. By focusing on what's important to each of us, working to compromise, and generally being open to others, the world functions reasonably well the majority of the time. What happens when someone believes they are special? What about if two individuals with Special Snowflake Syndrome disagree on a single topic? Do their heads explode? Kidding.

The point is that while we're all special and unique to ourselves and loved ones, we're all also **not** special to everybody else. Your perspective on any given topic can be just as valid to others, and definitely is to **you**, as anybody else's perspective, but in many situations it isn't actually any more important than someone else's. Remember what I wrote at the beginning of the book: if you find yourself uttering phrases like, "But I'm right" and finding yourself constantly arguing with people who disagree, you may want to take a hard look in the mirror.

Let's back up a step, though, and define exactly what we're talking about. Perspective has many definitions and, according to dictionary.com (n.d., para 1), two that are applicable are, "a mental view or prospect" and "the state of one's ideas, the facts known to one, etc., in having a meaningful interrelationship". So **my perspective** is basically my point of view on a given topic.

Perspective taking, then, is considering someone else's point of view. And usually when we're talking about doing it, it's someone whose point of view is, or appears to be, different from our own.

In the last chapter, I introduced the technique of **assuming benevolence**. This idea about giving someone the benefit of the doubt in the absence of any evidence one way or the other typically precedes the technique of perspective taking. In other words, step one is giving someone the benefit of the doubt and assuming they meant no harm with their words or actions. If I truly want to understand them, step two involves considering their perspective on the situation. I do this by gathering, or attempting to gather, evidence of what they're thinking and feeling. Keep in mind that if I am unable to gather evidence about their perspective, then I can stay with assuming benevolence. That way I'm still taking a positive or at least neutral stance.

One of the biggest roadblocks to considering someone else's perspective that I run into (whether in therapy or in "real" life), is the struggle someone has when they strongly disagree with the other person's perspective. This is quite likely to happen, and possibly often, to an individual with Special Snowflake Syndrome.

Immigration policy continues to be a huge issue in the United States. On one side, you have individuals who strongly believe that we have lax immigration policies and enforcement; on the other side, you have individuals who strongly believe that we need more open immigration policies, plus a number of people who have mixed opinions (Sanneh, August 2015).

Extrapolating from this debate, let's consider the following scenario. Mary and Sue are on opposite sides of an immigration rally. Mary supports full amnesty for all undocumented Americans whereas Sue would like a wall to be built along our southern border to stop all those illegal immigrants. Both hold signs championing their cause and are yelling at each other.

Why is it that they are overreacting to each others' stated positions? Why is it they seem unable to be respectful of each others' differences in opinion? Why are they unable to even try to consider the other's perspective? There's a very big reason:

Many people equate taking another person's perspective with either a) **agreeing with their beliefs** or b) **making excuses** for any disagreeable behaviors. Besides being incorrect, this misses the point.

A major point with taking another's perspective is that you **don't have to agree** with the other person. You just need to try to understand where they're coming from. Mary and Sue will likely never agree on immigration, but they can discuss it in a calm, respectful way, in part by trying to understand the other woman's perspective. This is known as empathy. It also may help to do so outside of a rally!

Taking another person's perspective is also **not done to make excuses** for inappropriate behavior. It's to understand what their motivation might be; if I want to be able to communicate in a helpful manner, then it's good if I at least try to discover their motivations.

Let's break this down a bit more.

What is empathy?

One definition of empathy is, "the psychological identification with or vicarious experiencing of the feelings, thoughts, or attitudes of another" (dictionary.com, n.d., para 1). In the simplest of phrasing, it means seeing things from another's point of view, or the old adage, walking a mile in another's shoes.

What role specifically does empathy have in perspective taking? Without question, it is the critical element. Trying to take another person's perspective without genuinely trying to understand their motivations will result in surface connection at best, and complete misunderstanding at worst.

Let's consider another example, this one from Chapter 3. Remember the story of the dueling Jesse Williams' petitions (France, 2016)? Mr. Williams gave a speech at an event that offended a bunch of people who demanded, by online petition, that he fired, prompting a bunch of other offended people to create their own petition in support of Mr. Williams.

How could the petitioners on both sides calm their special snowflake outrage by taking each other's, and Mr. Williams', perspective in this scenario?

The individuals who wrote and signed the petition demanding that Mr. Williams be fired can consider his motivations for saying what he did. Remember, empathy doesn't mean they have to agree. The actor said what he did at the event because it held meaning for him. If the individuals who wrote and signed the petition could recognize that Mr. Williams' is entitled to his opinion and that they don't have to agree with him, they could release the distress they feel.

On the flip side, those who then created the anti-petition petition could do the same. They can choose to consider the perspective of the original petition-creators. Both sides can recognize that, at the end of the day, by considering the motivations of all involved, they can let go of their artificially created distress. And hopefully learn not to be so reactive in the future to something that has nothing to do with them.

Although this is a simple example, it shows clearly how empathizing with the person we disagree with is critical to employing the technique of **taking the other's perspective** in reducing or eliminating a special snowflake's narcissism and childish expression of disagreement.

What is the goal?

An important component of empathizing with someone while trying to take their perspective on a thorny issue involves considering the purpose behind the interaction – both your goal and the other person's goal.

Why are you having the interaction in the first place? Let me tie that into taking others' perspective by returning a final time to the controversy at Yale University over the 'offensive' email regarding an adult's ability to choose their own Halloween costume.

To refresh your memory, a Yale University lecturer wrote an email essentially stating that college students were capable of selecting their Halloween costumes without being dictated to by the university about what was appropriate, with the result that some in the community demanded she and her husband resign because they, the students, no longer felt safe on campus (Friedersdorf, 2015).

How can we apply **taking the other person's perspective** to the special snowflakes in this scenario? As I suggested last chapter when we were **assuming benevolence** for the motivations of the lecturer, here we have an example where we can actively consider her goals in her interactions. How can we do that? Because she actually **told** her audience what her goal in communicating was, both in the initial email and in her later response to the special snowflake backlash. The hypersensitive students could have considered what the lecturer wrote and later said – she believes adult students are capable of picking their own Halloween costumes and responding appropriately if they see someone with a costume that they find offensive.

Note that normally I would encourage us to look at the perspectives on both sides, so that both can be reasonable, but honestly the lecturer and her husband, according to all accounts and the videos I've seen, were completely respectful in considering the students' perspectives (TheFire.org, 2015). They considered that the students were hurt by what was written and said, they were willing to meet with the students to discuss it, but unfortunately, the vocal students made it quite clear they had no interest in anything other than total admission of wrongdoing by the lecturer (and her husband).

Notice how neither side has to agree with the other in order to empathize? Both sides can consider the goals for the interaction. The lecturer clearly didn't agree with the students, but was willing and attempted to listen to them when learning of their distress. The students **could have chosen** to empathize with the lecturer and recognize her motivation for what was written. By taking the other person's perspective, they could have reduced their special snowflake overreactions, whether or not they agreed with the lecturer's opinions.

Seeking Validation

One common motivator that deserves special attention is the idea of validation of our opinions and ideas. It's so commonplace that it's likely hardwired in our brains to seek validation. Validation means "to make valid; substantiate; confirm" and valid means "sound; just; well-founded" (dictionary.com, n.d., para 1). Is it any wonder that people seek validation? I believe most people would like to be seen as knowledgeable and in-the-know. If we receive what we interpret as validation of our opinion, then that confirms for us that we're on the right track. It helps us feel like we belong with the group.

What does this have to do with Special Snowflake Syndrome and the **technique of taking another's perspective**? Consider the most relevant three of the eight symptoms I detailed in Part I: 1) elevation of their needs above others, 2) inability to recognize the perspectives of others or to consider that the opinions of others may have validity, and 3) easily offended by others' words and behaviors.

Individuals with Special Snowflake Syndrome are notoriously unable or unwilling to consider others' perspectives because they just don't care – their perspectives are more important and they are offended when others don't agree. Because they are narcissistically confident in their own opinions, they typically don't **seek** validation. Now, that's not to say they don't gravitate to others who agree with them. But, that's not for validation but for added power when they try to force others to agree with them.

A consequence of the special snowflake not seeking validation is that unless someone immediately agrees with them, they are unlikely to pursue it farther than that. **You don't agree with me; your opinion is wrong**. If they don't even try to have a genuine conversation with the person who holds an opposing view, it will be impossible to develop any kind of empathic understanding of where the other person is coming from.

The individual with Special Snowflake Syndrome may never get past the, "I'm right and you're wrong" stage if they don't try to take the other person's perspective. If the actual criteria of Special Snowflake Syndrome show that they may not be capable of doing it on their own, how can they learn to take another person's perspective? One way may be for the other person to take the first step.

Making the First Move

I read a fascinating blog on raptitude.com that indirectly talks about what I'm going to suggest next. It's something that I routinely hear from my patients in therapy and what I witness in my everyday life. In the blog post, the author writes, "the default is to treat strangers with indifference at best" (Cain, 2015, para 8). I would say it's broader than that.

Most, if not all, of us want the other person to go first. Doesn't even really matter the topic or context. If we meet someone new, we want the other person to introduce themselves first. If someone does something wrong, we don't want to forgive them until they first acknowledge they did wrong. Even if we love someone, we usually want the other person to say it first. Why is that? Self-protection, maybe. Fear of rejection? Desire not to be vulnerable? All of the above?

One way to help someone with Special Snowflake Syndrome who might not be inclined to consider the other person's perspective is for us to go first. Actually take the time to consider the special snowflake's perspective. And, if you are the special snowflake, work against your unhelpful narcissism, and try to be the one who goes first.

What would this look like? Throughout 2016, there have been numerous stories of tourists' actions resulting in the deaths of wildlife, including a goat, dolphin, and a bison (Klint, 2016; Tousignant, 2016; & Reuters 2016). With each reported death, there have been cries of outrage at the actions of the tourists. Remembering that empathizing and taking another person's perspective do not require agreement with the other opinion or action, how could the outraged readers **make the first move** by trying to understand the others' perspectives?

In each instance, the individuals involved did not know what the outcome would be. They did not have a crystal ball. Readers were outraged because in these cases, the outcomes were bad and the perceived motivation, especially for the two deaths due to selfie-taking, were even worse. So the first move the readers could take for the selfie-taking special snowflakes is to genuinely consider their perspectives.

Can you understand that when they saw, for example, a cute baby dolphin, they wanted to capture that moment? Can you empathize with the desire to snap what might have seemed a once-in-a-lifetime picture opportunity? This is probably challenging for you, again because of the outcome and perceived motivation (selfies are often a source of ridicule). However, if we want to help the special snowflake, then we can make the first move, by trying to understand their point of view, so that hopefully, they will then reciprocate and consider others' points of view about the situation.

Importance of Language

When it comes to helping an individual with Special Snowflake Syndrome to take another person's perspective, one important piece is language. Now, I don't mean in a special snowflake seeing-microaggressions-everywhere kind of way; but a true recognition that the way we talk to ourselves inherently impacts how we feel and what choices we make in our interactions with others.

Consider most of the scenarios I've presented thus far in this book, and even the special snowflake's internal dialogue itself. If someone uses inflammatory language internally, that will almost certainly reflect externally. In addition, if someone's not aware of this effect, it will be challenging to overcome.

In my practice as a clinical psychologist, I talk a lot to my patients about the filter we all have on the world. Every single person's filter is different. All of our experiences throughout our lifetimes mold and shape it. This filter becomes the prism through which we interpret the world around us. If your filter is 'clean' then you can see the world relatively accurately. When the filter is 'dirty' this results in distortions of how you see the world. These so-called **thought distortions** result in it becoming increasingly difficult to see another person's perspective.

Distorted thinking for an individual with Special Snowflake Syndrome begins, as I discussed in Part I, when society, particularly as expressed by parents, repeatedly tells someone that they are so special and unique that everyone will automatically support them and be on their 'side'. A special snowflake's filter will begin to develop the thought distortion of **being right**. With this distortion, the special snowflake begins to believe that just because they think or feel a certain way, that automatically makes it the right way.

The key with managing the thought distortion of being right is to remember that just because we believe it, doesn't make it true. And even if we're technically accurate, others still don't have to agree with us or see it our way. For a special snowflake, this seems like an impossibility.

Another thought distortion common for special snowflakes is **personalization**, or believing "that everything others do or say is some kind of direct, personal reaction to the person" (Grohol, 2015, #6). Essentially, the special snowflake tells themselves everything is about them; this contributes to the special snowflake symptoms of being easily offended and reacting in a childish manner, even to the point of extreme and inappropriate anger.

The key with managing the thought distortion of personalization is to remember that most things are not actually about us. In fact, people think or speak about us way less than our self-interest and narcissism tells us they do. How much time do you spend thinking about others? That's exactly my point. For a special snowflake, it seems inconceivable that they are not the center of attention.

These two thought distortions are reflected in both our internal and external language, clearly exemplified by the most dangerous thought distortion for individuals with Special Snowflake Syndrome, the danger of **"should"**. As I found perfectly written online, "we have a list of ironclad rules about how others and we should behave" (Grohol, 2015, #9). These are "should" thoughts. If at any time you utter the phrases, 'He should', 'she should', or 'they should', you are falling into "should" thinking.

The key with "should" thoughts is realizing that these are not rules, regulations, laws, or guidance that anybody **has** to follow. "Should" thoughts really just reflect our preferences. No more, and no less. And others are not going to necessarily share our expressed preference. This also seems impossible for the special snowflake and is often why disagreements deteriorate into temper tantrums, or efforts to force others to agree with them through attempted shaming or by using institutions to push others to conform against their will.

While there are other thought distortions, these three are the most salient for special snowflakes. Once we recognize these thought distortions, or succeed at helping a special snowflake to recognize them, then we can directly challenge such unhelpful ways of thinking and more actively consider others' perspectives through a 'cleaner' filter on the world.

Here's a politically-charged example to practice identifying personalization, being right, and "should" thinking, including translating them into **taking another's perspective** (note that this one is not ripped-from-the-headlines, but it did actually take place):

Crystal, a heterosexual woman, overhears Barbara, another heterosexual woman, speaking with Ron, a gay male, about Vicki, a female celebrity. Barbara and Ron wonder if Vicki is romantically involved with a woman with whom she spends a lot of time with, even though Vicki has not "come out" as a lesbian. Crystal expresses that this is inappropriate and she finds the conversation offensive.

Do you agree?

Let's change up the scenario a little bit. What about if Barbara and Ron were wondering if Vicki is involved with a male with whom she spends a lot of time with, even though she has never stated her sexual preference?

Would Crystal still believe this is inappropriate and offense?

If she did, would you agree?
And if she didn't, would you agree?

Here's the big question:

What is the actual difference between the two scenarios?

Both express curiosity about the romantic involvement of a woman in the public eye, a fairly common pastime for many. Why would one be offensive and the other not? And in fact, have you heard outrage expressed in the first instance, but not in the second? I definitely have. But, why?

Let's look at the perspectives of each:

One of the symptoms of Special Snowflake Syndrome is being easily offended, **especially if triggered by perceived injustice.** That is a key point to the above scenario. For many special snowflakes, even mentioning certain topics (race, sexual identity, gender) automatically triggers the assumption that what is being said is offensive and inappropriate. This is what the conservatives colorfully tend to call overreacting due to "liberal guilt" (for those unfamiliar with the term, when "people feel guilty for being born and/or raised in culturally, economically, socially or genetically favorable circumstances" from encyclopedia.dramatic.se, 2016, para 1). In my scenario, one could make the negative argument that Crystal is overreacting to the conversation due to her liberal guilt. But, if Barbara and Ron take her perspective, they could empathize with her expression of concern for a sensitive topic at greater risk for inappropriateness. Even if they don't agree with her.

For Crystal, on the other hand, she likely is responding to her perception of what liberals describe as "heteronormative privilege" (again, for those unfamiliar with the term, this denotes the perceived benefits of "a worldview that promotes heterosexuality as the normal or preferred sexual orientation" from oxforddictionaries. com, n.d., para 1). She could choose instead to take the perspectives of the two individuals having the conversation, actually listen to what is being said, and recognize that they were simply expressing curiosity. Even if she doesn't agree with them.

An interesting and educational experiment when it comes to language is changing the races, ethnicities, sexual identities/orientations, and/or genders in a story and see if you react the same way. If you don't, take a closer look and consider **why** you don't.

One final area under **Language** as it relates to **taking others' perspectives** is considering how we describe the scenario, whether before or after we empathize with someone. This is important because the way we typically describe scenarios is filled with judgment (positive and negative).

For this scenario, let's return to the class offered by the Office of Arts and Culture in Seattle, Washington on "White Fragility"; remember this term is defined as "the inability of white people to tolerate racial stress" (Quinn, 2016, para 4).

Would you label the above description as objective (free from bias) or subjective (based on evaluation)? I suspect the individuals who developed and promote the class, and possibly many of the individuals who have taken or plan to take the class, would describe that as objective. They likely see it as simply a definition.

But is it? For most folks, we're so used to describing scenarios from our own perspectives, filled with our own preferences and judgments, that we struggle to recognize that this is so, and in fact is not objective. Dr. Marshall Rosenberg (2003) has a helpful approach to communication that discusses the role of objective **observation** in **empathy.**

In the example above, the words chosen for the definition are inherently evaluative. The definition itself is evaluative. A result of this evaluation is that individuals are likely to be alienated by the language choices and true communication is shut down. As I wrote in the earlier chapter, while the intentions may have been positive, taking this approach will likely be interpreted as negative by many.

There is another option. Instead of choosing to describe the issues in evaluative ways, they could have chosen to use objective, observational descriptors. The creators/promoters of the class, in considering the **goal** of the class, could have chosen language that focuses on the objective behaviors they either would like to increase or decrease.

For those with Special Snowflake Syndrome, who likely struggle to recognize and comprehend that others could disagree with them, it may be particularly difficult to separate opinion from actual facts (this is where the refrain, "But I'm right!" comes from).

If those with Special Snowflake Syndrome and the people communicating with them could endeavor to consider the recommendations in this chapter to **take others' perspectives**, this would go a long way toward reducing several signs of the syndrome, namely 1) elevating their own needs above others, 2) inability to recognize the perspective of others, or to consider that the opinions of others may have validity, 3) being easily offended by others, and 4) believing that others are the sole source of any problem, negative emotion, or poor outcome.

On a broader scale, through increasing use of **taking others' perspectives**, we could unite and celebrate our differences if we recognize we're just like our neighbors, friends, and those who disagree with us. We just have different opinions.

Chapter Five Summary

Chapter 5 continued from assuming benevolence to perspective taking: considering someone else's point of view, especially critical when it's someone whose point of view is, or appears to be, different from our own.

Step one is giving someone the benefit of the doubt and assuming they meant no harm with their words or actions. Step two is to consider their perspective on the situation by gathering, or attempting to gather, the evidence of what they're thinking and feeling. Keep in mind that if I am unable to gather evidence about their perspective, then I can stay with assuming benevolence because I'm still taking a positive or at least neutral stance.

Taking others' perspectives does not mean you agree with them. You try to empathize with them, to understand where they're coming from.

Helpful considerations:

1. What is the goal in my interaction with another person?

2. Simply seeking validation or agreement is not taking the other person's perspective.

3. Recognize that someone has to go first in empathizing with the other – since individuals with Special Snowflake Syndrome struggle with this, it's likely to be the other person in the interaction.

4. Be aware of and work to reduce/eliminate the thought-distortions reflected in our language of "being right", "should", and personalization, both within ourselves and with the individuals with Special Snowflake Syndrome.

5. Focus on objective descriptions of scenarios instead of our judgments and opinions.

Notes

6 IT'S OKAY TO FAIL

I could have titled this chapter, 'It's okay to fail and/or not get your way'. Both of these are quite challenging and frankly unnerving for individuals with Special Snowflake Syndrome because they believe they are unique and deserving of special treatment, even in the absence of any actual reason. How could they possibly fail at anything?

Helicopter Parents Need to Land

In Part I, the role of parents in the development of Special Snowflake Syndrome was introduced. Specifically, I mentioned parents who want to be their child's best friend, tell them they can never fail, and assure them that the world will recognize their specialness.

Let's revisit that now, and actually define what that is, in part because it will help to explain why not just the

Millennials are developing the Syndrome.

What happens when you tell somebody that something is true over and over again? Let's say you're working at a company that just hired an employee. You take the new employee to lunch and repeatedly tell him or her how fabulous it is to work at Company Z. Even if you don't actually like working at the company that much, a funny thing starts to happen. You begin to believe what you're telling the new employee. You start to focus more on the positives you've been spinning for the new hire. In short, you drink the Kool Aid. It's exactly the same process with helicopter parents.

What are helicopter parents? A rather benign definition is "a style of child rearing in which an overprotective mother or father discourages a child's independence by being too involved in the child's life" (dictionary.com, n.d., para 1). A more snarky definition is, in part, "particularly prevalent at high-priced colleges, where parents feel obliged (or **entitled**) to intervene on issues down to the candlepower of the lightbulbs [sic]" (emphasis added, urbandictionary.com, 2005, para 1).

The second definition helps to explain how helicopter parents, by constantly feeling entitled to make sure that their little ones got everything their hearts desired, that the parents **also** were entitled to this treatment. As this began to spread from the parents to the children, and back, it also began to move to older adults. Then social media exploded it.

One huge step in curing Special Snowflake Syndrome then is for the individuals exhibiting the symptoms to first, recognize that it's okay to fail and second, that this means they don't need to come to anyone's rescue to make sure they are treated 'fairly'. Since one of the signs of Special Snowflake Syndrome is being **easily offended by others' words and behaviors, especially if triggered by perceived injustice**, an excellent step is to realize that just because someone fails or doesn't get their way, this is not, in and of itself, evidence of some kind of discrimination, or 'cause' that needs to be fought. It is perfectly normal to lose and not get your way.

Helicopter parents need to let their children scrape their knees, get told no, and fail at activities. Older adults need to stop expecting to get everything their way just because they have the wisdom of age. And, Millennials need to grow up and stop seeing injustice behind every statement they don't like.

Nobody Wins All the Time

Let's delve more into this idea that nobody wins all the time. Every single person on the planet has strengths and weaknesses. We all have things we're reasonably good at, hopefully some things we're awesome at, and likely some things we're terrible at. This is completely normal. What this means is that if I'm not good at a sport and I join a competitive league, it's unlikely I'm going to help my team win a championship. And that **used** to be perfectly fine.

Until it wasn't. In the age of the participation trophy, segments of society seem to have decided that winning and losing are archaic notions keeping everyone from being equal (Kurt Vonnegut wrote an amazing short story about this in 1961 titled *Harrison Bergeron*, available online). Let me be clear. While we can certainly debate ways to create a level playing field for starting, we will **never** achieve equality in terms of outcome because we are all different.

Not everyone agrees with me, of course. Some feel participation trophies teach commitment apart from success (Heffernan, 2015) and boost self-esteem (Pawlowski, 2013). Others agree with me that the age of the participation trophy might not have been the best choice (Grossman, 2015)

In the grand scheme of things, the participation trophy is likely not that big of an issue. The bigger concern is what it **represents**, and what it possibly teaches the youngest among us. Why do we want everybody to win and receive rewards like the participation trophy? What becomes our motivation for **why** we want to do things?

In psychology, we talk about **intrinsic** versus **extrinsic** motivation. This basically is the answer to the question, 'Do I want to do things for an internal reward like satisfaction, or do I want to do things for an external reward like a participation trophy?' If I do things for the sense of satisfaction it brings, then I may continue to engage in the behavior regardless of the input of others. On the other hand, if I engage in a behavior solely because of what I get from someone else, then I may find I lack motivation to ever engage in it **without** some kind of reward. I also may start to believe that I am **entitled** to receive something for all of my actions. And that brings us back to Special Snowflake Syndrome.

To reduce or eliminate some of the symptoms of the Syndrome, we must reduce the emphasis on always winning and/or receiving something external for our behavior. This will allow us to encourage development of internal motivation, such as from a sense of satisfaction, a desire for autonomy, or curiosity about the topic.

Remember we can't always win – and that's okay.

What is Offensive?

Related to the idea that it's okay to fail and not have people agree with you is this – sometimes people are offensive. It may be on purpose, it may be inadvertent, or it may be simply perceived as offensive. It's also, therefore, okay for people's feelings to sometimes get hurt. What is offensive to one may be perfectly fine to another. And unless you really want to police everyone's words, you take the good with the bad.

In a YouTube mini-documentary published by We the Internet on 7/16/2016, filmmaker Rob Montz discussed exactly this, in the context of Brown University's continued capitulation to what Mr. Montz labels "weaponizing victimhood" and "addiction to indignation". In the video, a university administrator at Brown University is quoted as saying learning is "the antithesis of comfort". Real debate cannot happen if we simply shout down the people with whom we disagree or attempt to shame them into quieting themselves.

In the comments section under the video, someone wrote, "The champions of tolerance now demand intolerance and see no double standard". This epitomizes the result of allowing those with Special Snowflake Syndrome to dictate to others, whether on college campuses, on social media, or in the general community.

The alternative is to recognize that sometimes we will offend. Sometimes we will be offended. Sometimes neither is true and someone is either misperceiving or overly sensitive. We decide in each instance what our response is going to be. For the individuals with Special Snowflake Syndrome, since **everything** they disagree with is liable to be labeled as offensive and they're likely going to have an overreaction to it, addressing that begins with recognizing the following:

It's okay for your feelings to get hurt.

It's okay for other people's feelings to get hurt.

If you prefer, don't hang around with people whose comments you don't like.

But understand that telling someone else how to live their life or how to speak 'appropriately' is not the answer.

Denial of Responsibility Language

The final section in this chapter that is directly related to the ideas that 1) it's okay to fail, 2) not everyone has to agree with you, and 3) offense is part of life, is **owning** each of those ideas when they occur. Individuals with Special Snowflake Syndrome do not own those – they point to others to blame if they fail; they denounce and ridicule others who do not agree with them; and they endeavor to shout down or restrict the free exchange of thought when they deem it offensive. All in the guise of their narcissism that **they** know best.

Individuals with Special Snowflake Syndrome can begin to get a handle on this by recognizing their use of **denial of responsibility** language (Rosenberg, 2003). We deny our responsibility for our choices – whether thoughts, feelings, or behavior – when we use language that puts the onus on someone or something else. Special snowflakes do this as a result of the symptom that they **believe others are the sole source of any problem, negative emotion, or poor outcome.** As a result of this denial of responsibility, the individual with Special Snowflake Syndrome consistently uses language that 'blames' others for all issues.

The alternative offered by Rosenberg (2003) is to replace that language with language that recognizes that we and everyone else have choices. Replace "I have to" with "I choose to". Every day and in every scenario, we choose what we want to do, how we want to respond, and how we want to feel.

For someone with Special Snowflake Syndrome, this seems completely foreign. They are enraged **because** others are not recognizing their greatness, or are disagreeing with them, or are not doing what they want. If they can be taught through education and modeling that ultimately they are only responsible for themselves – and that they are **truly** responsible (nobody else is responsible for their distress **or** their happiness) – they can begin to reduce some of the extremes of their Syndrome symptoms.

Think about those who have become phenomenally successful in their respective fields – Oprah Winfrey,

Tyler Perry, Jennifer Lopez, Anderson Cooper, Ellen DeGeneres – do you think they allowed anyone to **tell** them they could or could not do something? No, they went out and did what they wanted to do.

This has nothing to do with institutionalized racism, glass ceilings, and the like, and everything to do with how we choose to approach our challenges. Each person decides for themselves – blame someone else or double down to do what you want.

How do we do this?

For those with Special Snowflake Syndrome, ideally they can first be shown and encouraged to accept that not only is it **okay to fail**, it actually is a show of strength to own it when they do. Everybody fails if they're putting themselves out there. They can learn from every experience.

Second, those with the Syndrome can then be taught and shown that it's okay for others to disagree with them. This doesn't make the other person 'wrong', it doesn't mean the other person's words or actions are offensive, and it doesn't mean that there's some injustice that needs to be fought.

Third, learn to pick their battles. Part of the reason for the distress experienced by someone with Special Snowflake Syndrome is because it is simply exhausting to be offended and needing to right all the wrongs **all the time**. Learn to understand that some stuff's not that important and not worth the created emotional distress.

Finally, it's important for someone with Special Snowflake Syndrome to realize they **are not** always going to get what they want. Show them that instead of blaming others they can be responsible for their own success. And when they want to cry, "it's not fair", the appropriate response may be a little flippant, but cushioned with caring:

That's life cupcake. And that's okay.

It's okay to fail. It's okay for people not to agree with you. It's okay to not get your way. These are not necessarily negative things. They are all part of life. You are still you.

Chapter Six Summary

Chapter 6 brings several interrelated topics together: 1) it is okay to fail, 2) others do not have to agree with us, and 3) offense is a part of life. The key is to demonstrate to the individuals with Special Snowflake Syndrome that they can own these – and that ultimately only they are responsible for their thoughts, feelings, and behavior.

Helpful considerations:

1) Helicopter parents need to land (as do those who want to sweep in to rescue everyone) and let people fail.

2) Recognize that nobody wins all the time and that this is normal.

3) Just because you believe something is offensive doesn't mean it actually is, and unless it's crossing a legal line, people are allowed to be offensive (just don't hang out with them if you don't like it).

4) Watch for and change denial of responsibility language – individuals with Special Snowflake Syndrome do not own their thoughts, feelings, and behaviors – they point to others to blame if they fail; they denounce and ridicule others who do not agree with them; and they endeavor to shout down or restrict the free exchange of thought when they deem it offensive. Accept your responsibility and help special snowflakes to accept their own as well.

Notes

FINAL THOUGHTS

Special Snowflake Syndrome may only be an unofficial diagnosis at this point. However, in my clinical opinion and based further on my experience observing the world around me, it is going to increasingly become a problem. Something must be done to stop the continued individual, societal, and political damage. That was and remains my goal in having written this book.

As I stated in the **Introduction**, it is likely that most people reading this book will find something I wrote offensive. I deliberately picked inflammatory scenarios for many of my examples. If you found yourself uncomfortable or actually angry, that doesn't mean you have Special Snowflake Syndrome. Maybe I just hit on your particular primary issue or concern in the world.

On the other hand, if you or someone you know likely would have struggled with much if not all of this book, becoming angry and arguing with me continually…you or they might be a special snowflake. It's time to truly be the positive change I think most of us would like the opportunity to be in this world. Let's revisit the highlights of the book, from my definition of Special Snowflake Syndrome through the steps we can all take to reduce the symptoms – and save the world.

Part I: What is Special Snowflake Syndrome?

The label Special Snowflake Syndrome developed from the terms special snowflake and Generation Snowflake, and originally was simply a funny, disparaging comment used online to describe individuals who expressed belief they were unique, entitled, and special. Over time, all three terms gained traction and moved beyond the Internet to mentions in articles and books. Until now, however, nobody has written a book proposing that for a subset of the population, Special Snowflake Syndrome actually merits categorization as a personality disorder.

Special Snowflake Syndrome, as a proposed Cluster B personality disorder, would be potentially diagnosed in any individuals demonstrating a pervasive pattern of disregard for others, lack of empathy, grandiosity, and hypersensitivity, beginning by early adulthood and present in a variety of contexts. I specifically proposed eight criteria and would require the individual demonstrate five of the eight for diagnosis. Those criteria were:

1. Frequent demanding of special treatment regardless of circumstances.

2. Sense of entitlement or unrealistic expectation of favorable treatment from others regardless of deservedness.

3. Elevation of their needs above others, regardless of the objective importance of those needs, or the impact on others.

4. Inability to recognize the perspectives of others, or to consider that the opinions of others may have validity.

5. Easily offended by others' words and behaviors, especially if triggered by perceived injustice.

6. Displaying developmentally inappropriate behavior in response to perceived disagreeable actions of others.

7. Inappropriate and/or intense displays of anger, often in the form of a narcissistic rage.

8. Believes others are the sole source of any problem, negative emotion, or poor outcome.

As part of the chapter defining additional psychological features (e.g., diagnostic and associated features, prevalence) of the proposed personality disorder

Special Snowflake Syndrome, I detailed my theory for how the disorder formed and why it began with the Millennials (though won't stop there). In essence, what we are seeing with Special Snowflake Syndrome is that for a subset of the population: genetics predisposed them to self-interest; their parents shaped that self-interest to be exaggerated and unrealistic (and some of that ricocheted back on the parents); and, finally, social media seemingly confirmed their specialness and encouraged externalizing blame for all problems onto others. Society created Special Snowflake Syndrome.

After establishing the specifics of the diagnosis and the development of the disorder, the logical question may have been, so what? What impact does all this have and why should we care? In the final chapter of Part I, the reason why we should care was clearly outlined. Special Snowflake Syndrome is dangerous to the people with the disorder and even more dangerous to society:

As I expressed in Chapter 3, although Millennials seem to be the first to disproportionately demonstrate the Syndrome, it's not due to simple immaturity and youthful narcissism. They likely won't just grow out of it, or be the last, unless something is done to stop the continuation of their destructiveness, stop the creation of additional generations, and stop the formation of a tyrannical state that such individuals seem hell-bent on creating (for the greater good, of course!)

The dangers of Special Snowflake Syndrome thus begin first with dangerous psychological consequences for the individual. This then creates a bigger impact sociologically with dangerous negative consequences for society. Finally, all this pandering to the special snowflakes results in extreme political consequences, including the dangers of creating thought police or even a police state. What exactly does all this look like?

Special Snowflake Syndrome is creating a nation of self-perceived victims. The negative psychological impact of this on individuals cannot be overstated. Individual psychological dangers of Special Snowflake Syndrome creating a nation of victims include poor mental health and suicide, the tragedy of microaggressions, tyranny of safe spaces, and struggling with not always having their way.

For the individual with Special Snowflake Syndrome, when they elevate their needs above others, are unable to see another's perspective, display child-like behavior including temper tantrums or narcissistic rage, demand special treatment, have a sense of entitlement, and believe everyone else is the problem, they will be unable to look inward at their roles and responsibilities in their own life as well as the larger society, will be stuck in a perpetual state of being a victim, and will experience constant dissatisfaction with their own life as well as their functioning in society.

Moving beyond the individual, we see sociological consequences. Societal dangers of Special Snowflake Syndrome include individuals with the Syndrome aligning with others who agree that something is offensive, using institutions as weapons to drive out disagreements, and creating antagonism and animosity by sowing extreme divisiveness and discontent within the population from the disagreement.

Three dangerous political consequences follow from the above progression. The first is the ease with which we describe those that disagree with us in harsher and harsher terms, engaging in name-calling and trash-talking. The second is the progression to utilizing legal attacks, actually suing others for (in the loosest sense of the word) wronging us. What's even scarier than the name-calling and legal attacks is when this actually moves into changing rules, regulations, and laws. As a result of the societal consequences of Special Snowflake Syndrome detailed in this book, we restrict freedom in an effort to quiet the increasingly loud clamoring of every special interest group under the sun.

Having established *why* Special Snowflake Syndrome has dangerous far-reaching negative consequences for individuals and society, the second part of this book focused on reversing this dangerous trend, dealing with those already out there, and maybe even curing the Syndrome.

Part II: Curing Special Snowflake Syndrome

Chapter 4 introduced the first step in curing Special Snowflake Syndrome: assuming benevolence. This means that in the absence of any evidence, we choose to believe that someone's words or behavior were motivated by the desire to be kind. Or at the very least, we give someone the benefit of the doubt, choosing to believe neutral motivation. In order to do this, whether we are the individual with Special Snowflake Syndrome, or we are interacting with someone with the Syndrome, we ask ourselves, or ask them, to consider:

What is a possible neutral or positive motivation for the other person's comment or behavior?

Then we choose, or encourage the individual with Special Snowflake Syndrome to choose, to believe that alternative neutral or positive explanation.

Chapter 5 continued from assuming benevolence to perspective taking: considering someone else's point of view, especially critical when it's someone whose point of view is, or appears to be, different from our own.

Step one is giving someone the benefit of the doubt and assuming they meant no harm with their words or actions. Step two is to consider their perspective on the situation by gathering, or attempting to gather, the evidence of what they're thinking and feeling. Keep in mind that if I am unable to gather evidence about their perspective, then I can stay with assuming benevolence because I'm still taking a positive or at least neutral stance.

Taking others' perspectives does not mean you agree with them. You try to empathize with them, to understand where they're coming from.

Helpful considerations:

1. What is the goal in my interaction with another person?

2. Simply seeking validation or agreement is not taking the other person's perspective.

3. Recognize that someone has to go first in empathizing with the other – since individuals with Special Snowflake Syndrome struggle with this, it's likely to be the other person in the interaction.

4. Be aware of and work to reduce/eliminate the thought-distortions reflected in our language of "being right", "should", and personalization, both within ourselves and with the individuals with Special Snowflake Syndrome.

5. Focus on objective descriptions of scenarios instead of our judgments and opinions.

Chapter 6 brought several interrelated topics together, namely that it is okay to fail, others do not have to agree with us, and offense is a part of life. The key is to demonstrate to the individuals with Special Snowflake Syndrome that they can own these – and that ultimately only they are responsible for their thoughts, feelings, and behavior.

Helpful considerations:

1) Helicopter parents need to land (as do those who want to sweep in to rescue everyone) and let people fail.

2) Recognize that nobody wins all the time and that this is normal.

3) Just because you believe something is offensive doesn't mean it actually is, and unless it's crossing a legal line, people are allowed to be offensive (just don't hang out with them if you don't like it).

4) Watch for and change denial of responsibility language – individuals with Special Snowflake Syndrome do not own their thoughts, feelings, and behaviors – they point to others to blame if they fail; they denounce and ridicule others who do not agree with them; and they endeavor to shout down or restrict the free exchange of thought when they deem it offensive. All in the guise of

their narcissism that they know best. Accept your responsibility and help special snowflakes to accept their own as well.

Unfortunately, increasingly the perception is that we have become a world of special interest groups. I don't know that this is necessarily the case, or simply reflects the division seen in social media and on the news.

Certainly the individuals with Special Snowflake Syndrome will fit that mold.

Chanting,
"I'm special, recognize my specialness;
give me what I'm entitled to;
I'm offended, you can't say that!"

This adds to the negativity in the world. Consider all the dangers I detailed in Chapter 3, to the individual with Special Snowflake Syndrome, to the people around them, and ultimately to all of society through self-stylized thought police and restriction of freedoms. This is how the world might be if we do not heed the warning and act now.

Because it doesn't have to be this way. We can reverse our own special snowflake tendencies. And for those who would meet full criteria for Special Snowflake Syndrome, they can change too.

You are an individual, but so is everybody else.

You are not special. And that's okay.

We **can** save the world.

DR HEATHER SILVIO

FURTHER READING & RESOURCES

Almasy, S. (2014, January 13). Dad's texting to daughter sparks argument, fatal shooting in movie theater. http://www.cnn.com/2014/01/13/justice/florida-movie-theater-shooting/index.html

Almasy, S. & Visser, S. (2016, July 8). Live updates of the Dallas police shooting. Retrieved July 8, 2016, from http://www.cnn.com/2016/07/08/us/dallas-police-shooting-live-updates/index.html

American Association of University Professors. (2014, August). On trigger warnings. https://www.aaup.org/report/trigger-warnings

American Psychiatric Association: Diagnostic and Statistical Manual of Mental Disorders, Fifth Edition. Arlington, VA, American Psychiatric Association, 2013.

assume. (n.d.). *Dictionary.com Unabridged.* http://www.dictionary.com/browse/assume

Beaman, J. (2016, August 18). Princeton HR department: Don't use word 'man'. http://www.thecollegefix.com/post/28540/

benevolence. (n.d.) *Dictionary.com Unabridged.* http://www.dictionary.com/browse/benevolence

Bentley, L. (2014, March 10). Overcoming "Special Snowflake Syndrome" as a Millennial. https://medium.com/@leahbent/overcoming-special-snowflake-syndrome-as-a-millennial-2c3b83272e2b#.kcrg66j8c

Bowman, J. (2012, November 7). Republicans threaten move to Canada after Obama win. http://www.cbc.ca/newsblogs/yourcommunity/2012/11/republicans-threaten-move-to-canada-after-obama-win.html

Buckland, D. (2016, August 14). Social media culture damaging youth's mental health. http://www.express.co.uk/news/uk/699789/Celebrity-social-media-culture-youth-teenager-mental-health-selfie

Cain, D. (2015, April). The small habit that could save the world. http://www.raptitude.com/2015/04/small-habit/

Campbell, G. (2016, June 8). Yale English students demand 'safe space' from white authors like Shakespeare. http://politistick.com/yale-english-students-demand-safe-space-white-authors-like-shakespeare/

Campus Reform (2016, April 26). UMass Amherst students throw temper tantrum at free speech event. https://youtu.be/ANgl54duC0A

Carroll, L. (2016, April 28). So you want to move to Canada, eh? http://www.politifact.com/truth-o-meter/article/2016/apr/28/so-you-want-move-canada-eh/

Coulter, A. (2015). Adios America! The left's plan to turn our country into a third world hellhole. Washington, D.C.: Regnery Publishing.

Crocker, L. (2015, April 30). Britain's crazy decision to ban 'beach body' ads. http://www.thedailybeast.com/articles/2015/04/30/britain-s-crazy-decision-to-ban-beach-body-ads.html

DeSilver, D. (2014, June 12). The polarized Congress of today has its roots in the 1970s. http://www.pewresearch.org/fact-tank/2014/06/12/polarized-politics-in-congress-began-in-the-1970s-and-has-been-getting-worse-ever-since/

empathy. (n.d.). *Dictionary.com Unabridged.* http://www. dictionary.com/browse/empathy

Fincher, D (Director). (1999). *Fight club* [Motion picture]. United States: Fox 2000 Pictures.

Fox, C. (2016). I Find that Offensive. London, England: Biteback Publishing Ltd.

Fox News Latino. (2015, April 20). Report: 'Hamilton' creator Lin-Manuel Miranda calls out Madonna for texting during show. http://latino.foxnews.com/latino/entertainment/2015/04/20/report-hamilton-creator-lin-manuel-miranda-calls-out-madonna-for-texting-during/

France, L. (2016, July 5). Dueling petitions debate whether Jesse Williams should be fired from 'Grey's Anatomy'. http://www.cnn.com/2016/07/05/entertainment/jesse-williams-petitions/index.html

Friedersdorf, C. (2015, November 9). The new intolerance of student activism.

http://www.theatlantic.com/politics/archive/2015/11/the-new-intolerance-of-student-activism-at-yale/414810/

Frumin, A. (2014, May 14). Latest campus trend? Tossing out graduation speakers. http://www.msnbc.com/msnbc/college-commencement-speakers-backing-out-trend

Generation Snowflake. (2016, June 11). *Urban Dictionary*. http://www.urbandictionary.com/define.php?term=generation+snowflake

Grohol, J. (2015, October 6). 15 common cognitive distortions. http://psychcentral.com/lib/15-common-cognitive-distortions/

Grossman, E. (2015, July 25). How participation trophies are making our kids soft. http://www.mensjournal.com/adventure/races-sports/how-participation-trophies-are-making-our-kids-soft-20150725

Hadfield, J. (2016, May 26). DePaul Women's Studies department organises 'safe space' after Milo event. http://www.breitbart.com/milo/2016/05/26/depaul-womens-studies-department-organises-safe-space-milo-event/

https://www.thesun.co.uk/news/1436480/millennials-are-lazy-self-indulgent-and-lack-the-initiative-to-be-successful-warns-lifestyle-guru-martha-stewart/

hate speech. (n.d.). *Article 19*. https://www.article19.org/pages/en/hate-speech-more.html

hate speech. (n.d.). *Dictionary.com Unabridged*. http://www.dictionary.com/browse/hate-speech

Heffernan, L. (2015, August 31). In defense of participation trophies: Why they do really teach the right values. http://www.today.com/parents/defense-participation-trophies-kids-t40931

helicopter parent. (n.d.). *Dictionary.com Unabridged.* http://www.dictionary.com/browse/helicopter--parent

helicopter parent (2005, August 30). *Urban Dictionary.* http://www.urbandictionary.com/define.php?term=helicopter+parent

heteronormative. (n.d.). *Oxford Dictionaries.* http://www.oxforddictionaries.com/definition/heteronormative

Hume, M. (2016). Trigger warning: Is the fear of being offensive killing free speech? London, England: William Collins.

Iannello, K. (2016, August 8). Balanced presentation a dishonest exercise in presidential race. http://articles.philly.com/2016-08-08/news/74894017_1_republican-party-donald-trump-political-science

Kew, L. (2016, June 21). Twitter launches 'safe space' for celebrities. http://www.breitbart.com/tech/2016/06/21/twitter-launches-safe-space-for-celebrities/

Klint, C. (2016, July 18). Troopers: Mountain goat harassed by people drowns near downtown Seward. http://www.adn.com/alaska-news/wildlife/2016/07/18/troopers-mountain-goat-harassed-by-people-drowns-in-downtown-seward/

liberal guilt. (2016, June 21). *Encyclopedia Dramatica*. https://encyclopediadramatica.se/Liberal_guilt

Licea, M. & Italiano, L. (2015, December 18). Students at Lena Dunham's college offended by lack of fried chicken. http://nypost.com/2015/12/18/pc-students-at-lena-dunhams-college-offended-by-lack-of-fried-chicken/

Leopold, T. (2015, July 9). Broadway legend grabs phone from texter, laments future. http://www.cnn.com/2015/07/09/entertainment/feat-patti-lupone-cell-phone/index.html

Lopez, A. (2016, August 22). Poli-Sci prof says she must condemn Trump in class, calls balance an offense to the truth. http://www.thecollegefix.com/post/28570/

Marshall, M. (2016, August 25). New concerns arise about mental health of college students. http://boston.cbslocal.com/2016/08/25/new-concerns-mental-health-college-students-suicide/

McLaughlin, E. (2012, November 8). Election season bluster: Threats to move to Canada, a Trump call for 'revolution!' http://www.cnn.com/2012/11/07/politics/us-election-bluster/

McLean, R. (2016, May 2). Lawsuit says Starbucks' iced drinks have too much ice. http://money.cnn.com/2016/05/02/news/companies/starbucks-ice-lawsuit/index.html

Metaxas, E. (2016). If you can keep it: The forgotten promise of American liberty. New York: Penguin Random House.

microaggression. (n.d.) *Dictionary.com Unabridged*. http://www.dictionary.com/browse/microaggression

Moyer, J., Miller, M., & Holley, P. (2015, November 10). Mass media professor under fire for confronting video journalist at Mizzou. https://www.washingtonpost.com/news/morning-mix/wp/2015/11/10/video-shows-u-of-missouri-protesters-and-journalism-professor-barring-media-coverage/

Murphy, E. (2013, October 15). Fit mom defends controversial photo: 'I never called you fat'. http://abcnews.go.com/blogs/lifestyle/2013/10/fit-mom-defends-controversial-photo-i-never-called-you-fat/

Myall, S. (2014, March 15). 7 most ridiculous lawsuits: Nike, Susan Boyle, McDonald's coffee & outrageous cases that made it to court. http://www.mirror.co.uk/news/weird-news/7-most-ridiculous-lawsuits-nike-3238861

Nardi, W. (2016, August 15). Oregon State to force 'social justice' training on freshman. http://www.thecollegefix.com/post/28486/

Nash, C. (2016, March 3). Pitt students 'in tears' and feeling 'unsafe' after Milo Yiannopoulos event. http://www.breitbart.com/tech/2016/03/03/pittsburgh-students-in-tears-and-feeling-unsafe-after-milo-yiannopoulos-event/

Noren, L. (2011, October 4). Who is the Millennial generation? https://thesocietypages.org/graphicsociology/2011/10/04/who-is-the-millennial-generation-pew-research/

Nossel, S. (2016, June 3). To fight 'hate speech', stop talking about it. https://www.washingtonpost.com/posteverything/wp/2016/06/03/we-dont-need-laws-banning-hate-speech-because-it-doesnt-exist/

NYC Educator. (2009, November). Special Snowflake Syndrome. http://www.nyceducator.com/2009/11/snowflake-syndrome.html

Ohlheiser, A. (2015, October 7). Why 'social justice warrior,' a Gamergate insult, is now a dictionary entry. https://www.washingtonpost.com/news/the-intersect/wp/2015/10/07/why-social-justice-warrior-a-gamergate-insult-is-now-a-dictionary-entry/

Owens, E. (2016, July 12). 2016: Michigan State University faces civil rights complaint over women-only lounge in student union. http://dailycaller.com/2016/07/12/michigan-state-faces-civil-rights-complaint-for-women-only-student-union-lounge/

Palahniuk, C. (1996). *Fight club*. New York, NY: W.W. Norton.

Pawlowski, A. (2013, November 6). Should young athletes get 'participation trophies'? http://www.today.com/parents/should-young-athletes-get-participation-trophies-8C11542595

Pearlman, J. (2015, September 25). Facebook 'unfriending' can constitute workplace bullying, Australian tribunal finds. http://www.telegraph.co.uk/news/worldnews/australiaandthepacific/australia/11890275/Facebook-unfriending-can-constitute-workplace-bullying-Australian-tribunal-finds.html

perspective. (n.d.). *Dictionary.com Unabridged*. http://www.dictionary.com/browse/perspective

Peterson, H. (2014, January 20). McDonald's is getting sued again over alleged hot coffee burns. http://www.businessinsider.com/mcdonalds-hot-coffee-lawsuit-2014-1

Quinn, L. (2016, August 18). How to cope with 'white fragility': Academic sells out her $60 workshops designed to improve Caucasians' low emotional tolerance for discussing racism. http://www.dailymail.co.uk/news/article-3747572/Seattle-classes-white-fragility-sold-out.html

Reuters. (2016, May 17). Newborn bison had to die because of these dumb tourists. http://nypost.com/2016/05/17/tourists-try-to-help-bison-yellowstone-has-to-kill-it/

Richardson, K. (2016, April 11). Gay man severely burned in hot water attack: 'It was the worst night of my life'. http://www.wsbtv.com/news/local/atlanta/gay-man-severely-burned-in-hot-water-attack-speaks-out/168120996

Roebuck, J. (2016, August 19). Roommate drama lands Penn State sorority sisters in federal court. http://www.philly.com/philly/news/20160819_Roommate_drama_lands_Penn_State_sorority_sisters_in_federal_court.html

Roger, S. (2016). I know best: How moral narcissism is destroying our republic, if it hasn't already. New York, NY: Encounter Books.

Rosenberg, M. B. (2003). Nonviolent Communication: A Language of Life, 2nd Edition. Encinitas, CA: PuddleDancer Press.

Ruse, A. (2016, March 30). Jesuit university moves to fire conservative professor over his political views. http://www.breitbart.com/big-government/2016/03/30/university-moves-fire-conservative-professor-political-views/

safe space screamer. (2016, May 8). *Urban Dictionary*. http://www.urbandictionary.com/define.php?term=safe+space+screamer

Sanneh, K. (2015, August 19). A serious immigration debate, thanks to Donald Trump. http://www.newyorker.com/news/daily-comment/a-serious-immigration-debate-thanks-to-donald-trump

Shallwani, P. & MacMillan, T. (2016, May 13). Authorities drop hate-crime charges in Brooklyn Jewish school bus fire. http://www.wsj.com/articles/four-boys-arrested-in-connection-with-brooklyn-jewish-school-bus-fire-1463147537

Silvio, H. (2013). BabyBird Guide to Stress Disorders: A healing path for PTSD. Austin, TX: BabyBird Guides Ltd.

Soave, R. (2015, December 19). Oberlin College students: Cafeteria food is racist. http://www.thedailybeast.com/articles/2015/12/20/oberlin-students-cafeteria-food-is-racist.html special snowflake. (2015). *Know Your Meme.* http://knowyourmeme.com/memes/special-snowflake

special snowflake. (2015, November 24). *Urban Dictionary.* http://www.urbandictionary.com/define.php?term=special+snowflake

Special Snowflake Syndrome. (2011, March 20). *Urban Dictionary.* http://www.urbandictionary.com/define.php?term=Special+Snowflake+Syndrome

Starnes, T. (2016, June 27). Microaggression madness: Footwear flattery and Santa cause coed kerfuffle. http://www.foxnews.com/opinion/2016/06/27/microaggression-madness-footwear-flattery-and-santa-cause-coed-kerfuffle.html

TheFire.org (2015, November 6). Yale University students protest Halloween costume email (video 3). https://youtu.be/9IEFD_JVYd0

Torres, A. (2014, February 3). Microaggression. http://www.nationalreview.com/article/370078/microaggression-alec-torres

Tousignant, L. (2016, February 18). Selfie-taking tourists killed a baby dolphin. http://nypost.com/2016/02/18/selfie-taking-tourists-killed-a-baby-dolphin/

Truitt, B. (2016, August 12). Summer's civil war: How did pop culture get so negative? http://www.usatoday.com/story/life/movies/2016/08/08/summer-negativity-pop-culture-suicide-squad-ghostbusters-kanye-taylor/88329624/

University of Pittsburgh, Student Government Board. (2016, March). A statement regarding recent dialogue on campus by the 2015-2016 Pitt Student Government Board. http://sgb. pitt.edu/wp-content/uploads/2016/03/SGB-Letter-to-Students-March1.2016.pdf

valid. (n.d.). *Dictionary.com Unabridged.* http://www.dictionary.com/browse/valid

validation. (n.d.). *Dictionary.com Unabridged.* http://www.dictionary.com/browse/validations

Van Buren, A. (2016, June 18). Student pleads for help getting parents to co-sign for loan. http://www.uexpress.com/dearabby/2016/6/18/student-pleads-for-help-getting-parents

Vega, T. (2014, March 21). Students see many slights as racial 'microaggressions'. http://www.nytimes.com/2014/03/22/us/as-diversity-increases-slights-get-subtler-but-still-sting.html?_r=0

Volokh, E. (2015, May 7). No, there's no "hate speech" exception to the First Amendment. https://www. washingtonpost.com/news/volokh-conspiracy/wp/ 2015/05/07/no-theres-no-hate-speech-exception-to-the- first-amendment/

Vonnegut, K. (1961). *Harrison Bergeron.* http://www.tnellen. com/cybereng/harrison.html

We the Internet. (2016, July 14). Is the university killing free speech and open debate? https://youtu.be/ x5uaVFfX3AQ

ABOUT THE AUTHOR

Dr. Heather Silvio, a clinical psychologist, is the author of the self-help transformational program/book *Happiness by the Numbers: 9 Steps to Authentic Happiness,* the romantic comedy *Not Quite Famous: A Romantic Comedy of an Actress on the Edge,* the short story and poetry collection *Beyond the Abyss: Tales of the Supernatural,* the therapy book *The BabyBird Guide to Stress Disorders: A Healing Path for PTSD,* and the psychological thriller/murder mystery *Courting Death.* She is also an award-winning screenwriter, actress, and dancer. She lives in Las Vegas with her wonderful husband, Sidney, and their cat, Snowball.

To check out all this and more, as well as sign up for Heather's monthly newsletter, visit http://www.heathersilvio.com.

Please also visit
http://www.SpecialSnowflakeSyndrome.com
for more information and articles.